Construction Management

1

Organisation Systems

CW00373702

CONSTRUCTION TECHNOLOGY AND MANAGEMENT

A series published in association with the Chartered Institute of Building

The series covers every important aspect of construction. It is of particular relevance to the needs of students taking the CIOB Member Examinations, Parts 1 and 2, but is also suitable for degree courses, other professional examinations, and practioners in building architecture surveying and related fields.

Project Evaluation and Development
Alexander Rougvie

Practical Building Law
Margaret Wilkie with Richard Howells

Building Technology (3 volumes)
Ian Chandler
   Vol. 1 Site Organisation and Method
   Vol. 2 Performance
   Vol. 3 Design, Production and Maintenance

The Economics of the Construction Industry
Geoffrey Briscoe

Construction Management (2 volumes)
Robert Newcombe, David Langford and Richard Fellows
   Vol. 1 Organisation Systems
   Vol. 2 Management Systems

Construction Tendering
Andrew Cook

Adminstration of Building Contracts
James Franks

CONSTRUCTION MANAGEMENT

1

Organisation Systems

Robert Newcombe
David Langford
Richard Fellows

B.T. Batsford Ltd · London

in association with the Chartered Institute of Building

Typeset by Deltatype. Ellesmere Port
and printed in Great Brtiain by
Redwood Books, Trowbridge, Wilts

Published by B.T. Batsford Ltd
4 Fitzhardinge Street, London W1H 0AH

A CIP catalogue record for this book is
available from the British Library

ISBN 0 7134 6533 6

Contents

2 The Construction Environment   20

3 The Strategic System   41

4 The Organisation System 78

5 Information 115

6 The Social System 136

7 The Management System 170

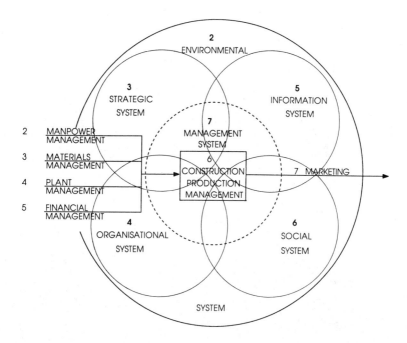

Figures in **bold** type above refer to chapters in this volume, those in light type to chapters in volume 2.

1 Systems Concepts

Construction organisations are notoriously difficult to manage due to the nature of the construction industry. Factors such as a fluctuating workload, prototype projects, a mobile and largely sub-contract workforce, regulatory bodies, government policy changes, etc, pose particular problems for the managers of building firms trying to apply sound management principles. Hence the description of the construction industry as characterised by the 'endemic crisis' suggested by the Tavistock Report (1966).

Managers need models which enable them to make sense of the apparent chaos outlined above – models which simplify the situation but retain a high degree of reality. Such a model is contained within *Systems Theory* which will be used as the basis of this book.

Before presenting a systems model of the building organisation, this chapter will review systems concepts and the systems approach, followed by the implications of viewing organisations as systems. A systems model of the construction organisation will then be used to present an overview of the whole book.

The definition of construction organisations adopted for this book is that of the construction contractor, mainly concerned with the production rather than the design of buildings and related structures. The historical dividing line between design practices and production organisations is becoming more blurred due to the increasing use of unconventional contract methods such as Management Contracting but, for the present edition of this book, remains. The managerial and organisational problems of professional design practices warrant separate consideration which is outside the scope of this book.

1.1 Systems theory

What do we mean by a system?

> There are many definitions of what constitutes a system. Basically any group of entities which are functionally interdependent can be called a system. Any group of entities which are interrelated so as to perform some function, or reach some goal, can be seen to be acting as a system.
>
> (*Open University 1974*)

The focus of systems theory is upon *sub-systems* which are *interrelated* in the pursuit of *goals* or *objectives*. The starting point for any analysis of a system is the definition of the *Primary Task* of the system. The Primary Task of an organisation as defined by MILLER and RICE (1967) is the thing it must do to survive. Architects must produce designs; building contractors must construct buildings at a profit.

Other important systems concepts are that:

(a) large systems comprise smaller sub-systems which work, preferably independently, towards the larger systems goals or Primary Task;

(b) those sub-systems form a hierarchy of systems, and by studying the inter-relationships of the sub-systems, we can understand the larger system;

(c) systems are 'open' because they interact with their environment. The environment affects the systems through constraints and imperatives but is not a part of the system because it does not share the goals of the system;

(d) the system receives inputs from the environment, applies some sort of conversion process and exports outputs to the environment;

(e) there is a permeable boundary between the system and its environment through which imputs and outputs pass. 'Boundary Management', or managing the interface between the system and its environment, is a key systems concept. These boundary management positions are usually very stressful. Boundaries also occur between sub-systems within a larger system;

(f) there is feedback when part of the output is fed back to become an input; thus a cycle of events is established which enables the system to monitor its own behaviour.

Systems Theory is more than just a set of concepts:

'I would suggest that the systems approach is a way of thinking which enables us to cope with complex phenomena by identifying their systemic relations. Once we realize that the structure we are studying displays the properties of a system we may be in a position to identify crucial goals, linkages or controlling factors in its structure and functioning. The analytical process typical of systems analysis can lay bare the interrelationships between sub-systems and their inputs and outputs, and may focus our attention on unexpected feedback loops, behavioural lags, delays in response to particular inputs, or crucial interactions between inputs or sub-systems. The systems concept ensures that we look for these linkages since we are aware that the structure we are studying is an interdependent arrangement of sub-systems.'

(*Open University 1974*)

This 'way of thinking' epitomises the approach of this book to the study of construction organisations.

1.2 Organisations as systems

How can organisations be analysed as systems?

Organisations clearly comply with the definition and concepts of systems theory given in the last section. They have identifiable goals, in practice multiple goals, and comprise interrelated sub-systems. The fact that these sub-systems contain human components introduces a degree of internal inconsistency within the system, but systems theory is able to cope with this 'people element' by focusing not on individuals but on the roles they perform in the system. Organisation can be defined as arrangements of people or roles. These roles within the sub-systems of the organisation are *formally* assigned to people or arise *informally* due to people's needs. Thus sub-systems may pursue goals which are contrary to the goals of the organisation, producing the multiple goals mentioned earlier. This may be compounded by the fact that the stated goals of the organisation may differ from the real operational goals. Organisations are large systems which contain a hierarchy of sub-systems in the form of functional departments and levels of management which work independently and interdependently towards multiple goals.

A study of the sub-systems, their human and physical components, and their interactions would facilitate a better understanding of the whole organisation. Such is the object of this book.

Organisations do not operate in a vacuum but within a particular *environment* with which they must interact to survive. Organisations are therefore by definition '*Open Systems*' which obtain *inputs* from their environment in the form of human, physical and financial resources, and export *outputs* to the environment in the form of products, services and, less tangibly, behaviour and attitudes. Equally, the environment applies constraints and imperatives to the organisation through political, economic, social and technological pressures.

Organisations receive *feedback* from their environment about the acceptability of their products or services, expressed, for example, in terms of purchasing patterns or financial support, which enables managers to make adjustments to inputs and the conversion process if they wish to respond.

Therefore organisations exhibit all the characteristics of open systems.

'The organisation, ie the whole complex of interrelated and encapsulated sub-units, groups and individuals, has to adapt to a changing world which includes other groups and organisations such as shareholders, customers, trade unions and governments.'

(Lupton 1971, p 122)

The concepts discussed so far can be illustrated using the input-conversion-output model shown in figure 1.1. This simple but powerful model will be used throughout the book and will be expanded in the next section by application to the construction organisation.

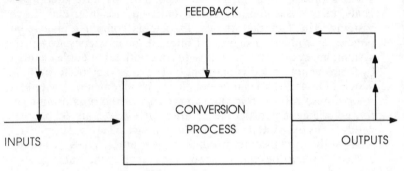

1.1　Input-conversion – output model

1.3　Construction organisations as systems

Construction organisations can be viewed as open systems and can be shown to exhibit all the characteristics of open systems. The definitive exposition of the characteristics of open systems was proposed by KATZ and KAHN (1966, 1978) who suggested that to understand organisations it is necessary to trace the input-conversion-output processes of the organisation, together with the feedback mechanisms which reactivate the system (see figure 1.1). Subsequent chapters of this book will analyse in detail the input-conversion-output processes of the various sub-systems of the construction organisation, but at this stage the ten characteristics of open systems identified by KATZ and KAHN will be used to examine construction organisations in a global way.

The following ten characteristics seem to define all open systems:

1　Importation of energy
'All organisations import some form of energy from the external environment' (KATZ and KAHN 1966)

Construction organisations receive inputs in the form of people – operative and management – materials, finance and, less tangibly, information. These inputs may be received from individuals or other institutions. Without this inflow of energy the organisation would die.

2 The through-put

'Open systems transform the energy available to them' (KATZ and KAHN 1966)

The construction organisation transforms the inputs, using various transformation processes. It creates new buildings and facilities, it processes materials, it assembles components, it trains people, or it provides a service. The majority of these conversion processes take place on the construction site, in response to inputs of design information and performance specifications. These are termed *operating* activities. In addition construction organisations carry out *maintenance* activities concerned with procuring and replenishing resources, eg purchasing, personnel and *regulatory* activities which relate various operating activities (sites) to each other, relate maintenance activities to operating activities (eg contracts management), and, most significantly, relate internal activities to the environment (MILLER and RICE 1967). It is this latter strategic management activity which is so frequently neglected in construction organisations, with disastrous results.

3 The outputs

'Open systems export some product into the environment, whether it be the invention of an enquiring mind or a bridge constructed by an engineering firm' (KATZ and KAHN 1966)

The output of the building firm may be a completed project, eg an office block; a product, eg building blocks; or a service, eg concrete testing. Equally the output may be a behavioural response by the firm's employees expressed in attitudes to the company or action against the organisation, eg strikes.

4 Systems as cycles of events

'The pattern of activities of the energy exchange has a cyclic character. The product exported into the environment furnishes the sources of energy for the repetition of the cycle of activities' (KATZ and KAHN 1966)

There is a feedback loop as shown in figure 1.1 which ensures repetition and continuity of the system. For building organisations this feedback will include contract payments for projects which will enable the company to purchase further inputs of labour, materials, plant, etc, in order to maintain building operations and leave a surplus for the shareholders. Often building is seen as a 'way of life' which implies that the outputs in terms of job satisfaction are in themselves sufficient to maintain the building company system's inputs even if financial rewards are small.

5　Negative entropy

'To survive, open systems must move to arrest the entropic process; they must acquire negative entropy. The entropic process is a universal law of nature in which all forms of organisation move toward disorganisation and death.' (KATZ and KAHN 1966)

The open system, by importing more energy from the environment than it requires for mere survival, or by exporting more outputs than are required to obtain inputs, can create organisational 'slack' or spare capacity. These 'reserves', which stem from the ratio of inputs to outputs, will enable the building company to survive a crisis and even live on borrowed time. Building firms actively seek to increase their spare capacity in order to improve their chances of survival. This may be in the form of capital investments or investments in resources. By this means organisations can almost indefinitely arrest the entropic process; nevertheless, the number of building organisations which go out of business every year is large. Entropy catches up with these firms.

6　Information input, negative feedback, and the coding process

The inputs to organisations are not only human, physical and financial resources but also *information* (see chapter 5), in the form of intelligence which provides signals about their environment and the organisation's position in relation to that environment. Construction organisations collect information about clients, competitions and contracts, for example, and use this to determine their bidding strategy for tenders.

They also collect information in the form of *negative feedback* which enables the firm to spot adverse trends and take corrective action to bring the organisation or the project back on course. This negative feedback could be declining profits at the corporate level or the increasing number of accidents on site, indicating a safety problem. The selection of inputs into the construction organisation is through a screening process called *coding*. Personnel will have certain criteria for employing people as will the purchasing department in selecting suppliers of materials.

7　The steady state

'The importation of energy to arrest entropy operates to maintain some constancy in energy exchange, so that open systems which survive are characterised by a steady state.' (KATZ and KAHN 1966)

The meaning of the steady state is the preservation of the character of the system. Construction organisations may increase in size and range of activities through increasing inputs and outputs but they are still basically in building; up to a point the character of the organisation remains the same.

In preserving the character of the system the organisation will tend to import more energy than is required for its survival (as discussed under 5 *Negative Entropy*). This results in growth and expansion to create a surplus or slack.

Another impetus to expansion is the way in which organisations adapt to their environment by seeking to control and/or incorporate external forces within their own boundaries, through backward and forward integration. For example, many building firms have bought up ready-mix concrete suppliers or ventured into property development in order to achieve greater control over the total building process.

The nature of growth is therefore initially quantitative, ie an increase in size, followed by qualitative change with the introduction of special supportive sub-systems which were not necessary when the organisation was smaller, eg Work Study.

Qualititative change also occurs as a direct result of an increase in size. A small building company which triples in size is no longer the same firm. Informal relationships will gradually be overtaken by creeping bureaucracy. Thus a new steady state will be established on a higher plateau of operation.

8 Differentiation

'Open systems move in the direction of differentiation and elaboration.' (KATZ and KAHN 1966)

It is clear from the previous section that increasing specialisation is a feature of growing organisations. Within construction organisations, differentiation typically occurs firstly by function, then by market sector, eg civil engineering, housing, etc, then by region eg national and international offices.

9 Equifinality

'According to this principle, a system can reach the same final state from differing initial conditions and by a variety of paths.' (KATZ and KAHN 1966)

The evolution of construction firms has been traced by a number of authors (CHANNON 1978, NEWCOMBE 1976, OGUNLESI 1984, O'CALLAGHAN 1986). CHANNON identified a range of construction business strategies differentiated by business diversification, acquisition strategy, international activity and internal versus external growth.

NEWCOMBE showed that it is possible to classify patterns of growth using a two-dimensional matrix with axes of diversification and geographical expansion.

All these studies illustrate that large construction corporations currently performing similar functions have arrived at their present positions by following different evolutionary paths, and from differing starting points, eg housebuilding, property development, civil engineering, etc.

Opportunities for equifinality may be reduced as organisations grow and move towards more standardised procedures: the 'creeping bureaucracy' effect.

10 Integration and co-ordination

As organisations grow there is a tendency towards increased differentiation or specialisation (see 8 above), followed by a complementary need for increased integration or co-ordination. As the structure divides, integration is increasingly needed. The necessary integration may be achieved by interpersonal contact in small organisations or formal procedures in larger, more bureaucratic, structures. The diverse range of inputs, activities and personnel involved in a typical building project poses a significant integration challenge. The lack of integration of the parties involved in a construction project has frequently been cited as a major cause of failure to achieve a successful outcome (EMERSON 1958, BANWELL 1964, WOOD 1975, NEDO 1978, 1983, etc).

At the corporate level there is also much evidence of the failure to integrate some of the key functions of the business, eg the purchasing department and the site, marketing and production, etc.

1.4 Closed versus open systems thinking

The foregoing are characteristics of 'open systems' but 'closed-systems' views of organisations still persist. Closed-systems views are evident in the failure to recognise that the organisation depends on inputs from the environment in the form of human and material energy and that the flow of such inputs is not constant. Traditional theories derived from this way of thinking focus on the internal functioning of the organisation and rely on tighter controls to achieve stability whereas, in a rapidly changing environment, flexibility may be more important (LANSLEY 1979). This has often resulted in contracting and professional firms taking a 'client be damned' attitude to projects and the omission of a consideration of environmental factors (as if they would go away if ignored). The recession of the 1970s happily brought an end to this attitude (amongst those firms who survived).

A second result of closed-systems thinking is the failure to appreciate the importance of 'equifinality' that there is more than one way of reaching a particular objective, and conversely that there is probably no 'best way'. Again, earlier 'universalistic' theories have been superseded by modern 'contingency' theories which suggest management and organisational solutions *appropriate to the situation* rather than 'best' solutions.

A third symptom of the closed-systems attitude is the 'failure to develop the intelligence or feedback function for obtaining adequate information about the changes in environmental forces' (KATZ and KHAN 1966). Many building businesses have been forced into bankruptcy as a result of a failure to monitor and recognise long-term changes in the construction markets in which they operated. Changes such as the rapid decline in public sector work, the increase in refurbishment-type projects and the switch to less conventional methods of contracting, eg management contracting, found many building firms unprepared.

The development of open-systems thinking is vital for managers of building companies to ensure the survival of their business. Systems models are not just another theoretical perspective but a practical tool for understanding the complexity of operating in the construction industry in the last decade of the twentieth century and beyond.

To summarise, the open systems approach is a way of thinking about organisation which sets out to:

1 *define the system*   This is done in two ways:
   (a) by a description of what the system is and what it does – the Primary Task;
   (b) by the establishing of the boundary of the system – what is inside and what is outside the system;

2 *identify the component parts of the system:*
   (a) the inputs to the system
   (b) the conversion processes which the system uses to transform the inputs into outputs,
   (c) the outputs of the system, both tangible and intangible
   (d) the feedback loops which complete the input-conversation-output cycle;

3 *define the environment of the system*, ie what is outside the system in terms of which elements impact on the system and vice-versa. The environment will consist of other organisational systems and the general environment. It is an understanding of the interactions of these systems which is the essence of systems thinking. The following section and the subsequent chapters will adopt this pattern of anaylsis.

1.5   Systems model of the construction organisation

A description of the construction organisation system was given earlier in the chapter, and so the starting point for this analysis of the system is a definition of the *Primary Task* of the system – the function it must filfil in order to survive. It is critical that the Primary Task is defined, as this determines the dominant input-conversation-output process within the organisation, identifies the operating activities (ie those activities that contribute directly to the Primary Task), and governs the allocation of scarce resources within the organisation.

The definition of the Primary Task is not easy. Within the organisation the Primary Task may be viewed differently by the corporate management and the managers and members of the comprising sub-systems. External stakeholders with an interest in the organisation may see the Primary Task of the business in a completely different way from the members of the organisation. In addition, a non-primary task such as personnel or marketing may temporarily become the Primary Task if the organisation needs to recruit engineers in large numbers or to win a prestigious contract calling for intensive marketing skills.

A compounding problem in defining the Primary Task is that it is often not explicitly stated but can only be inferred from the behaviour of the business.

In addition, the Primary Task of an organisation is affected by the internal culture of the business, in the form of its human and physical assets, and by the external environmental factors – political, social, economic and technical.

The construction organisation was defined earlier as the building contractor concerned with the production of buildings and related facilities.

The Primary Task of the construction organisation is therefore defined as:

> To obtain and execute construction projects to the client's satisfaction whilst meeting stakeholders' objectives.

This is the rationale for the existence of building organisations and what they must do to survive. They may offer other services to clients, or manufacture products, but their primary business is to construct buildings and related facilities.

The boundary of the construction organisation system, as with all organisations, is difficult to define, because the organisation is not a physical object but an abstraction in the minds of the members. One way of defining the boundary is to establish what is *outside* the system or, as stated earlier, 'is not part of the system because it does not share the goals of the system'. By this definition, clearly, the client, the professional team – architects, engineers, quantity surveyors, the material and plant suppliers, and arguably the sub-contractors employed – are outside the boundary of the construction organisation. By elimination, therefore, what is *inside* the construction organisation are those people directly employed and those assets actually owned by the firm. This would include building sites, which are temporarily 'owned' by the contractor for the duration of the contract.

Construction management systems

It follows from this definition of the Primary Task that the dominant input-conversion-output process is centred on the construction site. At the heart of a construction organisation is the building site. Therefore *construction production* is the dominant *conversion process* performed by building firms. Characteristic of the industry is that this process is unique, temporary and dispersed to a number of geographically decentralised sites. The greater part of the process is exposed to the climatic elements and conducted by teams especially assembled for the purpose. These multi-disciplinary teams are often from independent organisations, which led the Tavistock Institute (1966) to describe the nature of the relationship within the building team as one of 'interdependent autonomy'. The character of the conversion process creates a high degree of technical and social uncertainty amongst the parties involved, so that *interdependence* and *uncertainty* are key features of the construction production process (Tavistock 1966). The dominant *inputs* to this process are human, physical and financial. Construction is a people-centred and people-dominated industry whose craft processes and management practices have changed slowly.

The nature of the process just described means that mass production techniques or even robotics are unlikely to find wide-scale applications on building sites. People will be a prime, and increasingly scarce, resource for construction activity for the foreseeable future.

Construction is an assembly process requiring *physical inputs* in the form of materials and components. The materials and components are often bulky and heavy and whilst, in the past, large numbers of people were used to achieve remarkable feats of building, today the shortage of people has led to the development of sophisticated plant to carry out the heaviest tasks. The domination of the skyline of a construction site by a tower crane is a relatively recent phenomenon, as is the use of mechanical excavators and concrete mixers. The point is that these machines are able to achieve previously unattainable levels of production, but at a cost. They are expensive to buy and operate and even more expensive when they are *not* operating. The skilful management of plant both on and off the building site is crucial to the success of the modern building project. Building requires large capital investment and the flow of *financial inputs* to the business is critical to the survival of the building firm. Very few building firms can afford to fund the construction of buildings, and they rely instead on making contracts with clients in which the client will provide the main financial input.

This input is usually made in stage payments against the physical progress of the project, so that financial management skills of a high order are essential to ensure adequate cash flow to maintain the business. This financial flow is one of the key feedback components generated by the outputs of the building conversion process.

Within a growing construction organisation the early differentiation by function, described earlier, centres on the creation of *Personnel*, *Materials*, *Plant* and *Financial Management* roles to manage the human, physical and financial inputs to the business.

Given the Primary Task of the construction organisation, defined above, the tangible *outputs* of the construction conversion process are buildings and related facilities. The *Marketing* of these outputs is therefore a primary function of the building contractor. Again, a characteristic of the industry is that the product, ie the building, is usually sold before it is produced, which makes traditional marketing techniques, designed for the selling of consumer goods, largely irrelevant. These marketing techniques are appropriate for certain sectors of the industry, eg speculative housebuilding, but for the general building contractor constructing custom-designed building's there is little opportunity to market a product. It is, in fact, the intangible package of building skills which is the real output of the building firm. The physical output of the conversion process is a building, but the building contractor is really marketing the skills of planning and marshalling the resorces (or inputs), and managing the conversion process to a successful conclusion. Effective marketing forms once again a feedback loop, to enable the firm to obtain new contracts requiring fresh human, physical and financial inputs, thus maintaining the production cycle and the steady state of the firm. The input-conversion-output process of the construction organisation is shown in figure 1.2.

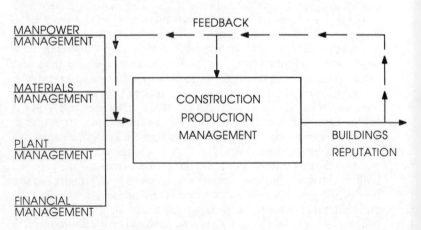

1.2   Construction management systems

Management Systems is the subject of Volume 2.

Construction organisation systems
As stated previously, the construction process shown in figure 1.2 is a temporary phenomenon. Construction projects have a life-cycle with a specific duration and a definite, if debatable, beginning and end. This temporary process occurs within the permanent infrastructure of the construction organisation, which comprises five interlocking systems as shown in figure 1.3. These systems form the environment or context for the construction conversion process and seek to facilitate and protect this 'operating core' from disruptive environmental influences (THOMPSON 1967). The five systems can also be viewed as open systems performing input-conversion-output processes. This is the approach adopted in the two volumes of work.

The **strategic** system performs the task of deciding and managing the long-term direction of the construction organisation. The strategic managers of the business receive inputs in the form of market intelligence, assessments of the firm's current capabilities

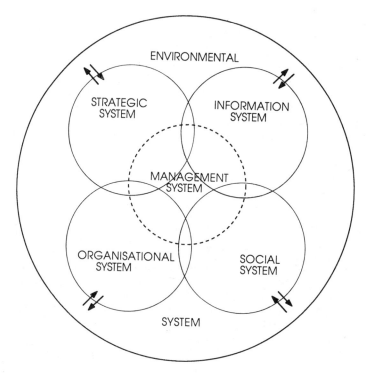

1.3   Construction organisation systems

and internal and external stakeholders' attitudes. These inputs feed a conversion process which decides objectives, generates optional strategies, evaluates, selects and communicates these strategies. The outputs of the strategic systems are strategic, administrative and operating decisions to facilitiate the strategies. A control loop ensures that feedback of results against plans is achieved to allow modifications to be made if necessary.

The **structural** system seeks to divide up or *differentiate* the work of the construction organisation in a rational way, and to *integrate* or co-ordinate the activities involved. The inputs to this conversion process are environmental and organisational characteristics, current activities and stakeholder attitudes. The outputs will be a formal organisation structure and an informal structure together with a complementary culture.

The **social** system's sole input is people of various types and levels. Through the processes of motivation, group formation, leadership and communication the system seeks to achieve an output of satisfied, committed and involved personnel.

The **information** system provides the lifeblood running through the arteries of the construction organisation. Information from sources external to the business, together with data from inside the firm, is collected, sifted, sorted and disseminated to the other systems in the form of time, cost, quality, resource and statutory data. Information may be formally documented or verbally disseminated.

The **management** system is shown in figure 1.3 as central to the whole organisational system. It occurs at three levels in the construction organisation – *strategic*, *administrative* and *operational* – each with distinct functions. The *strategic management* role has already been described under the strategic system. The *operational* management role has also been dealt with in discussing the construction production process. The *administrative* management role is usually referred to as middle management with responsibility for, in systems terms, maintenance and regulatory activities. At any level the management role involves making decisions, handling information and interacting with people. The way in which a manager fulfils the role will depend upon the inputs he receives through his perception of the organisation, the job itself, the team he works with and the task to be undertaken. His perceptions will be coloured by his own personality, preferred management style and the demands, constraints and choices within the job. The outputs of the management system are primarily decisions and actions, but providing a motivating environment to facilitate the implementation of decisions is equally important.

Construction organisation systems are discussed in this volume.

The environmental context

Just as the construction organisation system forms a context for the construction production system so the environment is the setting for building organisations. Building organisations operate within a multi-level environment comprising project, corporate, local, national and international levels. At each level many components and forces act upon the building organisation and this interaction between the organisation and its environment is one of the key concepts of Systems Theory, which is also covered in Volume 1.

1.6 Systems model and overview of Volumes 1 and 2

It is now possible to put these models together to form a composite systems model of the construction organisation as shown in figure 1.4.

This model is used to present an overview of the sequence of the chapters of the book through the two volumes, the contents of which will be introduced in this chapter.

Volume 1 Part A: CONTEXT contains this chapter, which explains systems theory and introduces two systems models together with a third model which combines the first two to give an integrated view of the construction organisation. Chapter 2 in this section will analyse the construction environment as a context for building organisations.

Volume 1 Part B: CONSTRUCTION ORGANISATION SYSTEMS contains five chapters dealing with each of the organisational sub-systems of the model in figure 1.4 – the strategic system (chapter 3), the organisation system (chapter 4), the information system (chapter 5), the social system (chapter 6) and the management system (chapter 7). The analysis of each system will discuss principles and practice. These five systems form the permanent infrastructure of the construction organisation. The dynamic process which building organisations undertake, and which is the rationále for their existence, is the subject of Part C.

Volume 2 Part C: CONSTRUCTION MANAGEMENT SYSTEMS also contains an introduction and five chapters which describe the management of the input-conversion-output process (see figure 1.2) for a construction organisation.

Chapters 2 to 4 of this volume will cover the management of the key inputs to construction organisations, namely, personnel, materials, plant, and finance. The treatment of these topics will not be exhaustive but will attempt to distil existing research and practice

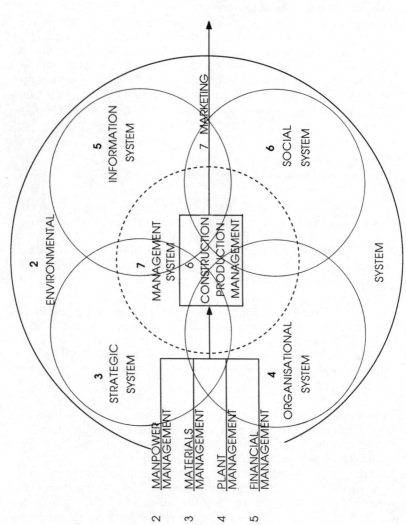

1.4 *A systems model of the construction organisation*

within the systems context. These are inputs which any construction organisation must obtain to ensure survival.

Chapter 6 is concerned with the core of all construction organisations – the construction production process which converts inputs into outputs. As with inputs, a 'strategic' rather than 'operational' view of this process will be adopted. The nature of the construction production process will be examined from first principles and the implications for managing the process both centrally and at site level will be analysed.

The last chapter of Volume 2 is concerned with the critical (but only recently recognised) function of marketing the outputs of the construction organisation. Again, the treatment will not be exhaustive, but will rather present an overview of the theory and practice of marketing within the construction environment described in chapter 2 of Volume 1. Whilst a substantial body of theory exists about marketing products, the greater part of it is not relevant to construction organisations; a selective approach is therefore essential.

Questions

1 Differentiate open and closed systems. Which model is more appropriate for construction companies? Why?

2 Identify five key characteristics of open systems giving examples of each from the construction industry.

3 'I would suggest that the systems approach is a way of thinking which enables us to cope with complex phenomena by identifying their systematic relations.'

Describe how the systems 'way of thinking' might help construction managers cope with the complexity of the construction industry.

4 Draw a systems model of a construction firm or building project. Explain the design concepts on which the model is based and how it might be used as a practical management tool.

2 The Construction Environment

2.1 Primary Task

The Primary Test is:
  To identify and to evaluate the independent, environmental variables which influence the activities of the organisation in order that the most favourable course(s) of operation may be pursued.

2.2 Environment

Every organisation operates in an environment; the environment is the context of the organisation's activities. Figure 2.1 shows that alternative levels of environment may be considered – the organisation includes the projects undertaken by that organisation, whilst the organisation's environment comprises local, national and international levels. As the level of the system being considered expands outwards from the centre (the project), the environment becomes increasingly general.

Inputs are provided by the environment, are converted by the organisation (system) and are returned to the environment as outputs. Some systems operate independently of their environment and thus may be considered as closed systems; other systems respond readily to events and occurrences outside the system, ie to environmental changes, and so form open systems. Open and closed systems are depicted in figure 2.2.

An open system has a boundary with the environment which is permeable, indicating that there is exchange between the organisation and its environment; there is dynamism in the system, particularly in the sense that the organisation responds to environmental forces and changes.

Although an organisation which operates as a closed system still takes resources and other inputs from the environment and, after conversion, returns outputs to the environment, it has an impermeable boundary in respect of the organisation's response to environmental changes.

Although elements of a production process operate as closed systems (eg a car body-panel press) it is not possible for an industrial or business organisation to be so isolated from its environment.

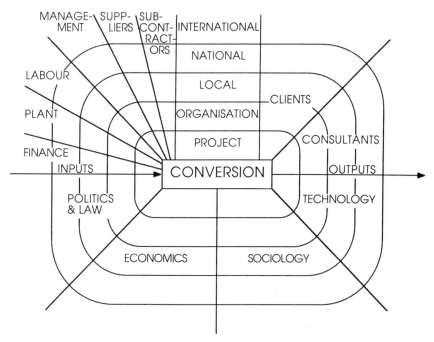

2.1 The environment

However, between totally closed and open systems lie intermediate forms; homostatic systems effect internal adjustments to cope with changes in their environments and so maintain equilibrium or remain static. Protected or semi-open systems defend themselves from their environments and so do not adapt fully in response to environmental changes.

It is important for an organisation to determine where its boundary lies and, hence, where the environment begins. Variables which are within the control of the organisation are internal, whereas those which are outside the organisation's control (exogenous) are environmental factors. Large and/or dominant organisations will be able to control a large spectrum of variables. It may be helpful for an organisation to classify variables into three groups:

- internal (endogenous): controllable
- environmental (exogenous): uncontrollable
- semi-controllable: those over which the organisation can exert some influence.

(The classification is analogous to that of economies of scale.)

It is inevitable that, to some degree, all organisations are fashioned by their environment. People form organisations; the circumstances in which people grow and develop are a primary

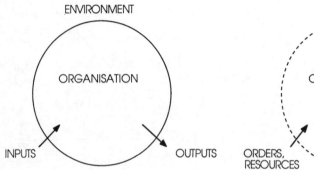
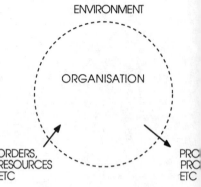

CLOSED SYSTEM   OPEN SYSTEM

ENVIRONMENT   ENVIRONMENT

ORGANISATION   ORGANISATION

INPUTS   OUTPUTS   ORDERS,   PRO
                 RESOURCES   PRO
                 ETC   ETC

IMPERMEABLE ORGANISATIONAL   PERMEABLE ORGANISATIONAL
BOUNDARY   BOUNDARY

2.2   Open and closed systems

influence upon them. Thus, organisations are reflections of history, their interactions with their environment determining how up-to-date and forward-looking they are.

The vast majority (if not all) of construction projects are open systems. Clients' requirements, briefs and project designs tend to be modified frequently – the project system must respond readily to the changes in order to be efficient. As construction organisations are a function of the projects which they undertake, there is a strong indication that, for success, the organisations must operate as open systems.

2.3   Internal structure

The environment, past and present, has been shown to be a major factor in shaping the internal structure of organisations. BURNS and STALKER (1966), from a study of the electronics industry, found organisation types to vary from mechanistic at one extreme to organic at the other. A mechanistic organisation is suited to stable conditions, managerial tasks are defined and broken down into specialisms, control is hierarchical with vertical communication and interaction emphasised, loyalty and obedience to superiors are required. An organic organisation is suited to unstable conditions – new, unfamiliar problems arise frequently and these cannot be broken into normal specialist functions or roles; adjustment of tasks and their re-definition are continuous, contributions from various specialists are featured, control is rather informal and communication ubiquitous; a high degree of commitment to the aims of the organisation is generated by the involvements required.

Most organisations lie on a continuum between mechanistic and organic and so exhibit degrees of both forms in a mix reasonably appropriate to their situation. (If this were not so, the inappropriately structured organisations would be inefficient and so go out of business.)

HANDY (1985) discusses four types of organisation culture – *role*, *task*, *power* and *person* – and relates them to four types of activity: *steady state*, *policy*, *innovation* and *crisis*.

(a)   Role culture organisation
Highly differentiated functions/specialities which are strong individually and separate from each other.
Control is by well-defined procedures and rules.
Co-ordination is effected by a small number of very senior managers.
Emphasis on roles/job descriptions rather than the people who perform those roles.
Power derives from position (job/role) within the organisation.
Efficiency is achieved via rational allocation of work and responsibilities.
Offers predictability and security.
Suited to stable environment, eg Civil Service; banking; insurance.

(b)   Task culture organisations
Project or job orientated, often as a matrix, seeks to combine appropriate resources and people to execute the project; very adaptable.
Control is difficult, retained by top managers and achieved through allocation of resources to projects, individuals have much control over their work.
Co-ordination by senior managers.
Emphasis on speed of response.
Power is not emphasised but influence is based on expertise.
Efficiency is achieved by appropriate resources and unifying power of group identity.
Offers individuals much control over their work, judgment by results and easy relationships.
Suited to situations requiring flexibility. eg advertising agencies; management consultants.

(c)   Power culture organisation
Strong organisations which can respond to threats rapidly but with centralised control; the central person's role is vital to success.
Control is centralised.

Co-ordination is from the centre, communication between functional sections is secondary to that with the centre.

Emphasis on centrality, selecting like-minded people to operate departments.

Power is from a central figure/entrepreneur.

Efficiency is dependant on the central figure and selection of departmental managers who have similar objectives and methods of operating.

Offers satisfaction to power oriented, risktakers who are politically minded; judgment by results.

Suited to environments which (may) pose threats, eg small entrepreneurial organisations; many 1960s property companies; some construction firms.

(d) Person culture organisation

Rather uncommon; the individual is the focus, any structure exists to aid the individuals.

Control is informal, no hierarchy exists.

Co-ordination is by co-operation.

Emphasis is on the people in the organisation.

Power, if required, is by expertise of the individuals in their subject-fields.

Efficiency depends on the individuals – their expertise and co-operating abilities.

Offers personal development and satisfaction.

Suited to various environments, depending on the people involved eg professional practices (partnerships); families.

  (i) *Steady state activities*
These activities are routine, often account for the majority of activities in an organisation, eg accounts, office services.

  (ii) *Policy activities*
These are concerned with overall direction, setting standards and ordering priorities, may involve allocaton of resources, eg directors forming a company plan, deciding what type(s) of project to undertake and for whom.

  (iii) *Innovation activities*
Concern changing what the organisation does and/or how it carries out those activities, eg R & D, marketing.

  (iv) *Crisis activities*
Involve dealing with unexpected events, eg production 'trouble-shooting', marketing, mid-management.

Thus, the form which an organisation takes, the activities which it pursues and the way in which it behaves, both internally and in relation to external factors, is dependent upon the organisation's culture and its environment.

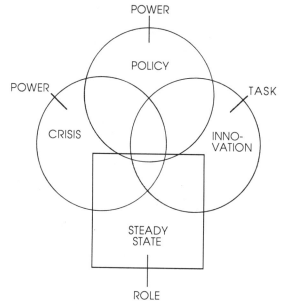

2.3 *Activity types and organisational cultures*

LAWRENCE and LORSCH (1967) suggested that as an organisation is a function of the nature of the task(s) to be executed and the environment; contingency theory is appropriate to the design of organisations. The suggestion is reinforced when the organisation's culture is taken into account also. Thus, there appears to be no one universally best way to structure an organisation but, given the environment, activities to be undertaken and the culture of those involved, certain organisational forms will be more appropriate.

The discussion is expanded in chapters 3 and 4.

2.4 Stability and turbulence

Environments themselves may be described in polar fashion, from stable at one extreme to turbulent (unstable) at the other.

In a turbulent environment change is continuous, often rapid and sometimes unpredictable. The changes may affect customers' values and behaviour and, thence, markets as well as technologies of production and products (or services). Therefore, there is little certainty over what outputs will be required, in what quantities and for how long. Of course, changes may be producer-generated through innovations designed to provide greater customer satisfaction. (For example, new materials and techniques being developed and employed to produce shorter construction times.)

Turbulent environments tend to be heterogeneous through time, and success in such circumstances requires flexibility, rapid response and innovation. Management and the management system of an organisation must be selected accordingly so as to thrive in the ambiguous situation of fluctuating goals and objectives.

In stable environments changes are rare and tend to be evolutionary rather than revolutionary. There are higher levels of certainty regarding the future and so planning is encouraged. Organisations which operate in stable environments can employ detailed and rigid systems for their activities and may even risk becoming a 'bureaucracy' which may be riddled with boredom and so reduced in efficiency. Such organisations are likely to be affected dramatically by a shock which alters the environment (rapidly and significantly).

Flexibility has costs, eg available capacity, stability has different costs, eg reduced efficiency due to boredom; excessive regulations. As the environments which are encountered show aspects of both turbulence and stability in various mixes, it is a vital task to design the organisation to suit the environment; often this will require the component parts of the organisation's being structured differently from each other.

(CLELAND and KING 1983) note THOMAS (1974) who suggested consideration of an organisation's 'environmental levels':

Internal environment – items which are within the organisation's jurisdiction and control.
Operating environment – other organisations, etc, with which the particular organisation deals directly.
General environment – national and international factors.

Again, with this model, the organisations control, influence and information diminish outwards from the internal to the general environments.

Figure 2.4 depicts THOMAS's environmental levels for an organisation; the model is adpated easily to show the situation of a project, a country, etc, as indicated by the levels of figure 2.1.

As environments form the context and exert major influences over the structure and operations of organisations, it is clear that the points of contact between the organisation and its environment are of primary significance to the organisation's success. Commonly organisations analyse their situations and future potential in terms of:

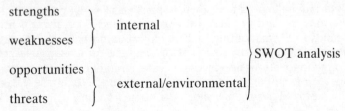

Strengths and weaknesses are internal – they are determined by the organisation. Opportunities and threats are external – they are outside the control of the organisation; are environmental factors to which the organisation must respond (even if by doing nothing).

Thus environments generate the main risks (statistically predictable events) and uncertainties (unpredictable events) for an organisation. The less stable the environment is, the greater the risks and uncertainties will be. The opportunities and threats which are generated continuously by a construction company's environment should be classified as risks or uncertainties as an initial step in their analyses; such an approach will assist the organisation in

ECONOMICS

2.4   *Environmental levels*

deciding future actions. (Much literature is available on the techniques of Risk Analysis and Risk Management.)

The degree of separation of an organisation's functional parts is determined, in large measure, by the nature of the environment. Often construction companies split their activities quite distinctly – many national building contractors 'regionalise' their operations; civil engineering and international work is undertaken by separate divisions; property development, plant hire and materials production are executed by subsidiary companies; and so on. Such separation occurs because the overall environment of the total organisation is very diverse and so is extremely difficult to analyse and respond to effectively at that level. The solution is to create a set of sub-organisations such that each operates in, and is structured to suit, a particular portion of the overall environment. Such disaggregation/specialisation is taken a stage further via subcontracting, etc.

The greater the degree of diversification within an organisation, and the greater the number of contributors to projects undertaken by the organisation, the more necessary and more difficult is the co-ordination of those diverse units to produce an integrated whole. Naturally the managerial requisites to achieve co-ordination and integration are different depending on whether the units to be co-ordinated and integrated are internal or external to the organisation. Dealing with external units is a more difficult task as, inter alia, they have goals and objectives which do not correspond with those of the organisation (see Tavistock Institute of Human Relations (1965)).

LAWRENCE and LORSCH (1967) found that the extent of differentiation in organisations which were effective was consistent with the demands exerted by the environment for interdependence of the parts of the organisation. Two studies of the construction industry (LANSLEY (1979), CHERNS and BRYANT (1984)) have reinforced the belief. CHERNS and BRYANT discuss construction project 'teams' as being Temporary Multi-Organisations (TMOs) in which the participants have varying and diverse objectives, requirements and loyalties which may (and frequently do) produce conflicts and thereby reduced operating efficiency for the project. Teamwork requires a large degree of commanality of objectives, usually involving sentience[1] and thereby yielding an efficiency of working via synergy.[2]

LANSLEY studied construction companies' fortunes through a

---

[1] *Sentience* – where people identify themselves to be members of a group, have common aims, etc, are loyal to the group and rely on it for both technical and emotional support; an essential facet of real teamwork.

[2] *Synergy* – the whole is greater than the sum of the parts (the 2+2=5 effect); the result of good teamwork.

period of recession and concluded that flexibility was an essential ingredient for survival. Whilst it appears justified to describe the construction industry as conservative, it is also clear that the pace of change (technology, project procurement systems, etc) is increasing. The result is a necessity for constructors to be more flexible in order to accommodate the changes rapidly.

BENNETT (1985) found that successful organisations were those which were 'strong' at their points of contact with the environment, especially where the environment posed threats to the organisation. Strength does not imply merely being able to respond to and overcome threatening situations but also the ability to seize and take advantage of opportunities; again demonstrating the need for flexibility.

A critical factor in determining the strength of an organisation at its point of contact with the environment (and for shaping the nature of the organisation, notably its degree of flexibility) is the people involved. Ownership and management determine strategies and tactics at and from the centre but the tasks of everyday representation of the organisation and actions vest in many and various employees (sales staff, site agents, forepersons, etc).

In considering the situation of management contracting and the use of sub-contractors, etc, it is helpful to consider two forms of environment which are external to the organisation (the management contractor) as illustrated in figure 2.5. The major environ-

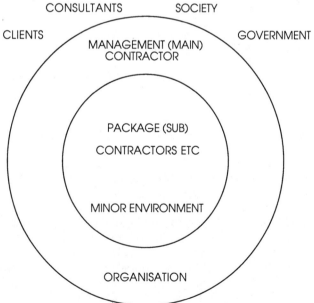

2.5 *Major and minor environments*

ment comprises the external environment of the organisation, as shown in figures 2.1 and 2.4. The minor environment is subject to influences from the organisation but retains independence. Contacts with and influences of the two environments are different and occur in different ways through different personnel; both are important and it is a potentially serious error to regard and to treat the minor environment as being 'internal' to the organisation.

2.4 Elements of the environment

Figure 2.1 depicts a classification of environmental factors and levels. The levels – *International*, *National*, *Local*, *Organisation* and *Project* – indicate environmental boundaries and, hence, likely influence and control. The top half of the diagram comprises factors which may be regarded as fairly specific whilst those factors in the bottom half of the diagram tend to be more general in their natures. The north-east sector of the diagram constitutes demand and its expression; the north-west sector represents resources used to meet the demand; the southern sectors represent generally pervading factors which affect both demand and supply (often termed PEST factors).

Demand factors

Clients
Clients comprise public sector and private sector organisations; individuals (potential and actual householders) are the clients of housing developers.

Public sector clients are central government; local government; public authorities such as the National Health Service and public corporations such as the BBC; plus firms, industries and other bodies in public ownership such as British Steel and water authorities (much privatisation of this sector has occurred during the 1980s).

The mechanism by which the public sector expresses demand to the construction industry is by 'limited interpretation'. Initiation of demand is by a perception and quantification of need. Once quantified, various needs are ranked to produce an hierarchy and decisions on which needs to meet, how and to what degree, are taken within the limitations of available funds (the sizes and distributions of which often are decided by Government and, hence, are subject to political considerations). The result is expressions of demands for projects to the construction industry – new build, rehabilitation and refurbishment, and repairs and maintenance.

The public sector is the foremost client (by far) of civil engineering organisations; in building, there has been a marked downward trend in demand from the public sector, particularly since the late 1970s. The suggestion that Government uses the construction industry as a regulator of the economy seems to have considerable substance.

Private clients are organisations and individuals within the private sector of the economy. For industrial and commercial organisations their expressions of demand for building work are derived from the demands for their own outputs – buildings are viewed as a particular type of resource used in production (factor of production). That buildings are fixed assets, the stock is large relative to the flow of new buildings, production of buildings takes time and is subject to derived demand indicates that the accelerator principle applies (see HILLEBRANDT (1974)).

Particularly in city centres, it is normal for the clients for commercial buildings to be property development companies. Such companies assemble sites, arrange finance – often from institutional investors – commission the building and then lease the building to tenant-users. Similar development arrangements are occurring for industrial premises, notably in respect of 'industrial parks' although in this sector owner development and occupation is still common.

It is rare for individuals to commission bespoke houses from a building company; the common mechanism for housing provision in the private sector is by housing developers constructing (usually estates) for subsequent sale. Here the trigger for production is demand for houses as perceived by the housing developer. Housing developers usually own several tracts of land in various locations (often called 'land banks'), all of which have planning permission for housing; development occurs, clearly, as and when the developers deem it to be most profitable; the price of land is determined by the price of (in this case) the finished housing on the market and NOT vice versa. (See, for example, HARVEY, J (1988).)

Clients may be classified as a continuum from *naive*, the client who builds once or very seldom and so has very little knowledge of the industry, to *expert*, the client who builds frequently, employs construction personnel and has much knowledge and experience of the industry. Most public sector clients plus developers and large commercial and industral 'chains' constitute experienced clients; multi-national companies often have vast experience of construction projects overseas. The nature of the client is important to contractors for their marketing, client involvement in controlling projects and performance requirements to achieve client satisfaction. Roles and influence of consultants also depends upon the type of client.

Expert clients tend to be less susceptible to certain marketing efforts of contractors, eg literature to promote design and construction activities, more involved with the production of projects (both design and construction phases) and more demanding of performance (notably multi-nationals which may easily make international performance comparisons). To some extent the additional demands imposed by expert clients may be mitigated by their knowledge of the industry's systems of operation – what can be demanded reasonably, what information is required when, etc. Such clients tend to be coveted by contractors as they may offer repeat orders and larger projects, some of which may be rather complex.

Consultants
Architects, Structural (Civil) Engineers, Services Engineers and Quantity Surveyors are the usual consultants on a building project. Recently, further consultant titles have emerged, the most prominent being the Project Manager – someone who acts as the manager of the whole project (or a major part of the project) for the client. Frequently, the Clerk of Works (CoW) is not a consultant but is employed by the client directly; the CoW's task usually is to act as inspector of the construction to ensure compliance with the specification, etc, under the direction of the Architect – it is often the case that the practical powers of the CoW greatly exceed the theoretical (or contractual) powers, especially on public sector contracts.

Most consultants' primary functions are concerned with design – the translation of clients' requirements into drawings, schedules, specifications and other documents from which buildings may be constructed. Further functions concern obtaining contractors to execute the construction and various aspects of the construction to secure performance to meet clients' needs.

Due to individualities, diverse loyalties and similar effects which detract from true teamwork, the process of provision of a building may be depicted as in figure 2.6. Several interpretation/filtration

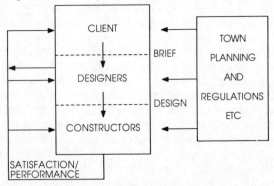

2.6 Simple model of the process of building provision

processes occur; the well-known and significant difficulties of communication are also present, most notably at transmission of information between different parties.

Traditionally, the architect has assumed a triumvirate of roles – designer of the building, manager/co-ordinator of the total design functions and manager/controller of the construction on behalf of the client. Engineers' roles have tended to be secondary – designing the structure and services for the building to suit the architect's overall scheme, plus some (usually ex-contractual) specialist supervision of construction, eg inspecting reinforcement, etc, prior to the concrete being placed, and control functions (eg checking applications for interim payments). The quantity surveyor provides cost advice (cost planning) during design, advises on contractual matters, produces a bill of quantities on which contractors tender (if appropriate) and provides post contract financial control (although the architect certifies payments, etc) and contractual advice.

Guidance to the services available from consultants and standard conditions of engagement are published by the various institutions to which most consultants belong. Fee scales are no longer applicable and consultants now bid for work. (This bidding requirement may create difficulties, especially for novice clients, in deciding the best value bid – what elements of the proposed consultants' services are required and what is a reasonable price for those services, ie which bid represents the 'best value for money'?)

Although it is popular for consultants to consider themselves as impartial professionals in their work on building projects, it is becoming increasingly clear (and necessary) that they act on behalf of their client, notably regarding disputes and claims – the architect no longer can be regarded as a quasi-arbitrator.

For common arrangements for engagement of consultants and their functions see, for example, *Clients' Guides*, CIOB; *Plan of Work*, RIBA.

Resources

The resource inputs noted in the north-west sector of figure 2.1 are discussed in detail in chapter 7 of this volume and chapters 2 to 5 inclusive, of Volume 2.

General environmental factors

The southern half of figure 2.1 comprises the general environmental (PEST) factors of Politics and Law, Economics, Sociology and Technology. WALKER (1984), and other writers, advocate consideration of cultural, ethical and institutional factors also.

Politics

Politics is the 'science' of State organisation, affairs of State and, perhaps most practically, questions of policy. It has been suggested that politics is the art of the possible but it may be more appropriate to adapt a well known quotation concerning statistics to: 'There is truth, there are lies and there is politics'. Politics is a factor not only of central and local government but also it pervades all institutions and organisations – it is a process of attempting 'manipulations' of people's behaviour in striving for the particular ends which the 'politician' desires.

For governments, electoral considerations frequently are paramount and, whilst such factors do not affect most managers, directors of companies and officials of various organisations (such as trades unions) may be subject to elections from time to time. Hence self-promotion to achieve popularity, and thereby secure (re-) election, is important to many politicians, as the position to which they are elected is one which commands power, so enabling them to implement their policies.

The science or art of elections is complex but two facets are worthy of note. First, for electoral success, it may well be preferable to ensure avoidance of policies which may prove to be unpopular rather than to concentrate on potentially popular policies alone. Second, the process of 'logrolling' – assembling a set of policies on a variety of issues designed so as to secure the votes of (diverse) groups of voters who feel strongly about those issues, taking care that the policies do not contain major conflicts – is a mechanism for collecting votes.

As politicians, particularly those in office in central and local government, determine policies and actions on many issues – monetary policy, fiscal policy, employment, industrial development, rating, etc – it is hardly surprising that many individuals, groups and organisations seek to influence policies to further their own interests. Construction is amongst such lobby groups. Lobbying occurs not only overtly by letter, discussions and other communications between the interest groups and politicians but also it occurs covertly through such mechanisms as organisations contributing to the funds of the favoured political party.

In the late 1970s and early 1980s the construction industry's 'Group of Eight' – comprising representatives of major organisations in the construction industry – was an unsuccessful overt lobby group. However, in the mid to late 1980s overt and covert lobbying by construction and development organisations, it appears, has achieved considerable success, notably in securing releases of land in the south east of England for housing developments despite counter-lobbying by local anti-development groups. Such releases often have been secured by appeal to the Secretary of State following refusal of planning permission by the local authority. (Notably it has been common for all the parties involved to be of similar political persuasion.)

Generally it is acknowledged that planning issues are not a major electoral consideration (from the viewpoint of what influences people's voting); this, probably, is true also of expenditure on both new construction and renovation, repairs and maintenance. Housing provision does seem to form somewhat of an exception to the generalisation although some circumvention of the impact of policies concerning provision of housing in the public sector has been achieved by the enforcement of sales of local authority housing during the 1980s.

The construction industry is affected by a large number of political factors, perhaps most notably regarding economic, employment and industrial policies.

Law

The two primary forms of English Law are statute (law enacted by Parliament) and judicial precedent (case law). The industry is involved with applications of planning law, development control (Building Regulations, Factories Acts, etc) and law of property, as well as the more general areas of contracts, torts, sale of goods and supply of services, and limitation.

The law provides a general framework for and prescribes boundaries within which people's actions occur, whether as individuals or on behalf of others or of organisations. The law is the ultimate arena for the settlement of disputes (litigation); arbitration is a less 'officious' mechanism which is designed to be cheaper and quicker than litigation. The powers of an arbitrator are different from those of the courts, the former being documented in the arbitration agreement.

Although, within certain limits, parties may enter into contractual relations about whatever they choose and on whatever terms they desire, the construction industry favours the use of standard forms of contract, eg ICE 6th edition; JCT '80. In recent times forms of contract have proliferated to accommodate an increasing variety of methods of procuring construction work. The situation also has resulted in standard forms being adapted for individual circumstances together with greater use of non-standard contracts.

The legal environment is becoming increasingly complex daily. Everyone is deemed to know all the law; ignorance of the law is no excuse!

Economics

The economic environment is determined largely by the policies of the UK Government, foreign governments, plus international traders and (capital) speculators. In particular, fiscal and monetary policies are important – fiscal policy concerns patterns of government expenditure and income; monetary policy concerns the supply of money and credit facilities, notably rates of interest.

Fiscal policy effects the industry directly through its effects on the demand for new buildings and works, whilst monetary policy has indirect effects, particularly through changes in the rate of interest (increases reduce the demand for construction and make construction more expensive).

A simple model of a governed, open economy is:

$$Y = C + I + G + (X - M)$$
$$Yfc = Y - Ti$$

where?

Y	=	National income at market prices
Yfc	=	National income at factor costs
C	=	Consumption
I	=	Investment (= S = Savings)
G	=	Government expenditure
X	=	Exports
M	=	Imports
Ti	=	Indirect Taxation

People's take-home (disposable) income is either saved or spent. In the simplest economy, savings = investment so $Y = C + S = C + I$. If (a) represents the proportion of disposable income which is saved (marginal propensity to save) and (b) represents the proportion which is spent on consumables, if there is an addition to investment of ΔI, then the change Y due to ΔI is:

$$\Delta Y = \Delta I \frac{(1)}{1-b}$$

A multiplier $(1/1-b)$ operates, which for the UK economy approximates (in either direction, positive or negative) to almost 2. The multiplier applies to employment also.

As the construction industry produces long lived assets (investment goods, subject to derived demand), annual additions to which form only a very small percentage of the total stock at the time, the industry is suceptable to the accelerator effect. Further, although the construction industry obtains much of its inputs from a few other industries, no other industry, at least in the short term, derives much of its average inputs from construction.

The above factors, and the labour intensive nature of the construction industry, have meant that governments have been able to use the industry as a mechanism for assisting regulation of the economy. A mitigating factor is that, due to the industry's methods of working (quite long periods of design and construction), effects of regulatory policies have been subjected to time-lags and smoothing, eg, moratorium on local authority housing which occurred in 1980.

As construction is a relatively high risk industry and a market (nominal) rate of interest comprises risk, time-preference (together = real rate of interest) and inflation, it follows that the cost of capital to contractors will be relatively high. The normal methods of interim payments mean that construction projects are good generators of cash but, due to the competitive situation prevailing in the later 1970s and in the 1980s, they are not very profitable activities. However, even with very low profits-on-costs, due to the quite low capital investments required (through plant hire, sub-contracting, etc), the profits expressed as return on capital employed are of the order of 2½ to 3½ times the profits on costs. (The situation is discussed further in chapter 5 of Volume 2.)

The international economic environment affects not only the prices of imported materials and goods, eg timber, tiles, but also the relative competitiveness of UK construction organisation (contractors and consultants) bidding for work overseas (a high pound makes these UK exports more expensive). Relative rates of inflation between economies are important also. In bidding for international work, the attractiveness of the financial package which the bidder can offer is frequently the factor which is critical in assessing the bids. The roles of the banks (merchant and commercial), Government agencies (notably the Export Credit Guarantee Department) and the bonding worthiness of the bidding organisation are fundamental factors in the international construction market.

Sociology

This sector most appropriately contains culture and ethics as well as sociology; it concerns how people behave, their values and, so, forms the social context for construction activities and organisations.

People, individuals and groups, constitute resources for construction (see chapters 6 and 7 and Volume 2 chapter 2) and the essence of demand for construction whether by expression of demand directly or via an 'interpretive medium', such as the Health Service, responding to an assessed, perceived need.

People determine whether buildings are constructed, what buildings are produced, where, why and how. Urban development and the forms of buildings are functions of societies. Some building forms have strong bases in religious beliefs. Many modern towns have basic patterns of layout determined by ancient societies (Roman roads, etc). Thus the present stock of buildings has evolved and reflects past as well as current societies.

In international development, countries and societies which came under the control of imperialist nations (mostly of Western

Europe, eg the UK) had the social values, styles and forms of the colonising nations forced upon them. Only recently has the damage caused by such an approach been acknowledged actively and the modern means of assisting development is to provide aid programmes suited to the recipient country, notably in the provision of *appropriate* and *sustainable* technology rather than 'high technology'.

The society of a country and/or its 'coloniser' is fundamental in the determination of that country's laws and legal system. Far Eastern countries, Islaamic nations, Western countries and 'Communist' countries all operate differently both domestically and in business – the societies are different as manifested by their laws, values and societal structures (consider the 'institutions' in a society, who and what are revered?).

Technology
Technology is a basic determinant of what and how the industry can build. Also, technology determines where it is possible to construct – dewatering, ground stabilisation, foundation engineering, etc. Generally technology advances so the range of construction possibilities increases, indeed the rate of advance appears to be in the form of geometric progression.

Technology affects productivity; often major increases in productivity are associated with technological advances, notably increased/more efficient use of plant. Changes in technology require investment; because people are reticent to invest when the future is perceived to be uncertain, investment by the construction industry has been rather sluggish.

Various reports (eg, RICS (1979)) indicated that the UK construction industry performed poorly in comparison to foreign counterparts. Although the differing levels of performance could be attributed, in part, to varying development controls, safety provisions and industrial organisation systems, an important factor was the technologies of construction which were employed. It is a popular belief that technologies which are used in USA are adopted about ten years later in UK.

A significant force for the adoption of updated technology to increase efficiency of construction is the demands of clients, particularly commercial developers and other experienced clients; knowledge of performance levels achieved abroad is influential on expectations of what the UK industry should achieve. The results are not only changes in techniques of construction but also in specifications to facilitate adoption of new techniques (eg power floated finish to a concrete slab instead of a screed). Such changes are facilitated by an approach of performance analysis for the finished building to determine what is required rather than 'blind' adoption of historic requirements, norms, standards and specifications. The increasing inputs of construction expertise to design (via design and build, management contracting and project management systems) enhance this new and more realistic approach to the determination of what the requirements of the finished building are. Analyses of projects in the NEDO (1983) study demonstrated that it was more likely that time could be saved during the design of a project than during its construction, despite the potential for some alterations in the construction technologies used. It is, indeed, often the case that alterations of the system of production will yield greater efficiencies than will changes in the techniques of production within a given system.

Certainly in recent times a primary force for contractors ensuring that their systems and technologies are up to date and efficient, is the mechanism of competitive tendering used to award work. It may be that with the advent of competitive bidding amongst consultants for design will result in their increasing efficiency also (provided clients are equipped adequately to evaluate competing bids for design, etc, which are likely to offer different services and levels of service as well as varying levels of fees for those services).

For an analysis of processes used in architectural practices see MACKINDER and MARVIN (1982).

2.6 Risks and uncertainties

Strictly, risks are events, the probabilities of the occurrences of which are statistically predictable; uncertainties are unpredictable. Thus, whilst risks may be allocated to the parties who have the best opportunities to control the risks and so act as incentives for improved performance, due to cost considerations, it is likely to be most efficient for uncertainties to reside with the client.

In the construction industry, forecasts of performance are deterministic – normally based on detection of trends and their extrapolation. The predictions are usually single figure estimates which may be taken to imply accuracy which does not exist. Other industries, such as oil and petroleum, employ stochastic (probabilistic) forecasting techniques and so their forecasts contain measures of variability, thereby conveying more realism.

As construction projects advance, environmental risk factors alter – the risks and uncertainties are still present but the potential effects of adverse factors change. Also, the power and influence of the numerous parties involved with a project to make and to implement decisions vary with the project stages. Naturally organisations which operate in different environments and circumstances are subject to different risks and uncertainties.

Generally the response to risk assumption by a contractor is to increase the bid to compensate; there is also the bid's probability of success to be taken into account. In terms of environmental risks (and uncertainties), the need is to balance the costs of employing 'contingencies' (eg exceptionally adverse weather precautions) to deal with those risks and the costs which would result if the risk events occurred. A marginal cost approach should be used – increase the contingency until its marginal cost equals the incremental risk-cost saving.

Thus it is evident that prediction plays a fundamental role in risk management – what risks are present, of what sizes, to whom allocated and what are the responses? The objective is to take action to mitigate potential detrimental effects subject to the organisation's operating requirements.

Questions

1 Describe the economic and legislative factors which influence the design team and contractor throughout a building project from inception to completion.

   CIOB *Building Technology II* 1987

2 Explain, using examples, how the conflicting needs of society may have to be reconciled when determining the most suitable built environment for the future.

   CIOB *Building Technology II* 1987

3 'It is no measure of success if an organization meets its financial targets but fails to meet its social ones.' Sir Peter Parker, former chairman of British Rail.
   Discuss the applicability of this statement to a building company.

   CIOB *Building Management II* 1986

4 Evaluate the contention that, in order to be successful, a building contractor must operate as an open system.

3 The Strategic System

The Strategic System is the system which determines the long term direction of the organisation. It therefore comprises a decision making process and a management role. The system generates strategic decisions which are made by the strategic management system (see chapter 7). It is traditionally assumed, because of the nature of strategic decisions, that the strategic system is synonymous with the role of chief executive or board of directors. Whilst this is entirely true in some organisations, eg small firms, and partially true in most organisations, the strategic system is much more dispersed within the building company.

The strategic system operates wherever in the organisation strategic decisions are made. In order to trace the extent of the strategic system it is necessary first to define and establish the characteristics of strategic decisions.

ANSOFF (1965) was one of the early writers who defined strategic decisions as 'primarily concerned with external, rather than internal, problems of the firm and specifically with selection of the product mix which the firm will produce and the markets to which it will sell'. ANSOFF recognised two other classes of decisions, **operational** and **administrative**, which are affected by and influence strategic decisions. These three classes of decisions are the outputs of the strategic system but an appreciation of the characteristics of strategic decisions is fundamental to an understanding of the strategic system and will be dealt with here.

3.1 Strategic decisions

The characteristics of strategic decisions:

(a) they are concerned with the *scope* of the organisation's activities – the extent of diversification of services and markets, and the degree of forward and backward integration, eg forward integration for builders could be into property development, backward integration could involve purchasing a brick-making or ready-mix concrete supplier. In system's terms, strategic decisions define the *boundary* of the organisation, that is the interface with the environment. The decision to move into property development or purchase a ready-mix concrete supplier, effectively shifts the boundary of the organisation so that an activity which was formally outside the organisation is now an integral part of the company;

(b)   they seek to match the organisation's activities with the **environment** in which it operates. More specifically, to match the strengths and weaknesses of the firm to the opportunities and threats in the market place. In a rapidly changing environment, such as exists in the construction industry, this implies that if a match is to be maintained then strategy needs to be constantly reviewed. A mis-match between strategy and environment may have disastrous consequences for building organisations particularly during a downturn in demand, a lesson many contractors learned to their cost after 1973;

(c)   they seek to match the firm's activities to the capabilities of the organisation and to its resources. There is little point in considering property development unless the building firm has, or can obtain, the necessary finance to purchase land and fund development. The firm's capabilities obviously determine its strengths and weaknesses;

(d)   it follows that another feature of strategic decisions is that they have major resource implications. They commit the organisation to changes in the use of its existing resources or to obtaining additional resources. The decision to introduce computing into the business will entail re-training of existing staff to use the new systems or the appointment of new staff;

(e)   they will affect operational (project) and administrative (business) decisions as pointed out by ANSOFF. This will be discussed under outputs later in the chapter;

(f)   they will be affected by the expectations and values of the key stakeholders in the business. These people may be inside or outside the organisation, but a common feature is that they exercise power through the control of resources. This will be discussed under inputs;

(g)   strategic decisions are complex because there is always present a high degree of uncertainty about environmental forces and outcomes. This will also be discussed under inputs;

(h)   a final characteristic is that strategic decisions affect the long-term direction of the organisation. Decisions made to-day will have long-term implications for the business for years ahead. This is the key indicator which distinguishes a strategic decision from other sorts of decisions which firms have to make – that they have an *impact on the whole organisation*.

We are now able to define the *boundary* of the strategic system as anywhere or anyone in the organisation, if the decisions made exhibit some or all of these characteristics. More specifically any decision at any level in the business which impacts on the whole organisation is a strategic decision. Conversely any decision which does not exhibit any of these characteristics, even if taken by the chief executive, is *not* a strategic decision but a tactical decision.

3.2 Levels of strategy

It follows that strategies will exist at a number of *levels* in the organisation.

(a) The first is at the **corporate** level; here the strategic decisions are concerned with the businesses or markets that the company should be in. They are decisions about **scope**. This level of corporate strategy will only occur in multi-divisional or holding company businesses. Corporate strategy involves decisions about the organisation as a whole.

(b) The second is at the single **business** level within the corporation. *Business strategy* is about how to compete in a particular market. Units at this level are frequently referred to as Strategic Business Units or SBUs. Typical SBUs in a building organisation would be house building, civil engineering, building, joinery, concrete blocks, property development, etc.

(c) The third level of strategy is at the **operational** or **project** end of the organisation. Decisions by heads of functional departments – estimating, buying, plant, etc, and decisions by managers of construction projects often impact on the whole business. For example the chief estimator's decision on pricing strategy for a major contract and the method decisions taken by a site manager may bankrupt a building firm and sometimes do. This is because individual projects represent a large proportion of a building contractor's turnover and, therefore, profit.

The *boundary* of the strategic system will occur at any of these levels. The *process* of making strategic decisions is termed *strategic planning* and the *responsibility* for formulating and implementing strategic plans rests with the *strategic management* system in the business (see chapter 7.)

3.3 The primary task

The Primary Task of the strategic system is:

" to match the organisations capabilities with opportunities and threats in the environment to achieve competitive advantage. "

This definition highlights the crucial contribution that the strategic system makes to the health of the building organisation. The activities involved are shown in figure 3.1.

3.4 A systems model of the strategic system

From figure 3.1 it can be seen that the **inputs** to the stategic system are *market forces* and *organisational forces*.

The *conversion process* requires the strategic managers to set the *objectives* of the organisation or project, generate *optional* courses of action for achieving the objectives, *evaluate* the options, *select* what is considered to be the best option or options to pursue, and *communicate* the selection decisions to the relevant people for action.

The **outputs** of the strategic systems will be *strategic* decisions and *administrative* and *operational* or *project* decisions to facilitate the implementation of the strategies.

The ultimate result should be **competitive advantage.** It is crucial for success in a highly competitive industry, such as construction, that the building organisation exhibits some advantage over its competitors in the eyes of the customer or client. Strategies for achieving competitive advantage will be discussed.

Feedback will come in the form of success or otherwise in meeting the desired objectives. This will need to be monitored through a *strategic control* system.

The way in which the strategic system operates will depend upon the *strategy making mode* adopted by the strategists. The choice of mode by strategic management will be discussed.

3.5 Inputs

1 Market forces
If any organisation is to survive and prosper it is critical that the opportunities and threats that the environment poses are recognised or identified. The general nature of the construction environment has been discussed in chapter 2; this section will be concerned with the impact of the peculiar features of the construction environment on the building firm and the kind of market information which is likely to have a bearing on strategic decisions.

There are a number of steps involved in environmental analysis to gain market information as shown in figure 3.2.

(a) Auditing environmental influences
The environmental influences on building organisations have been identified in chapter 2, figure 2.1, in terms of general and specific influences together with the levels of the environment which exist –

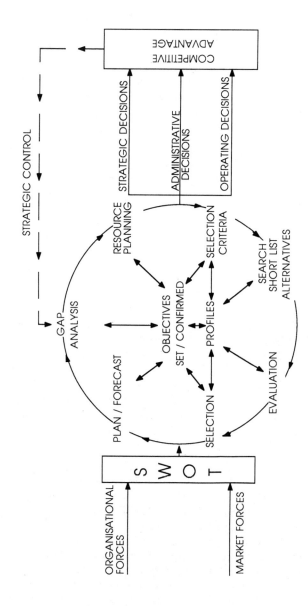

3.1   A systems model of the strategic system

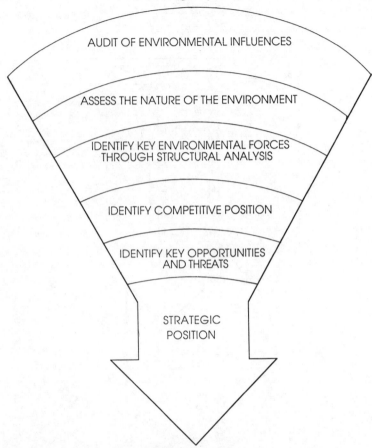

3.2   Steps in environmental analysis

project organisation, local, national and international. As indicated in chapter 2, the southern elements of the figure are often common to all firms in a particular environment. For example, all firms operating in the United Kingdom face a broadly similar political, economic, social and technological environment in contrast to those operating in another country.

It is important for strategic management to audit trends in these forces and assess the implications for the firm. Typical trends which are likely to affect building organisations are the movement in interest rates, the decline in public sector projects, a decrease in the birth rate, the number of graduates from universities and colleges, the development of robotics, the decisions about nuclear power, the rise in crime, etc.

And increase in interest rates, for example, usually has a direct effect in depressing demand for construction projects, particularly speculative housing. Equally, a change in policy towards criminals may require more prisons to be built.

Of the specific environmental influences shown in figure 2.1, those in the northern hemisphere of the figure, will have more direct effects on the building organisation. There are two groups to be monitored:

(i)   the *buyers* of the firm's services, eg the clients and consultants. Market research is an essential activity to obtain information about clients' construction intentions and consultants' commissions.

(ii) the *suppliers* of services to the building contractor, eg material suppliers, sub-contractors, plant hire companies, financial institutions, etc.

Proper procurement procedures and records are essential – some large contractors have national computer-based data banks of this sort of information. These suppliers of services are often an early source of information about the purchasing intentions of clients and consultants. Buyers and suppliers form two important components of the *competitive environment*.

(b)   Assess the nature of the construction environment
As stated in chapter 2, environments range from stable to turbulent in nature.

Changes in the nature of the construction environment have been charted by LANSLEY (1979) over three decades.

1960 to 1970 was a period of gradual if fluctuating growth in demand with a healthy public sector workload providing relative stability.

1973 was a watershed year when the oil crisis precipitated a 25% drop in demand for construction in a single year and heralded a recession which created tremendous turbulence in the building organisations environment. Flexibility was the key to survival during this harrowing period.

The 1980s have brought another boom in construction demand but again created a turbulent environment because of shortages of resources, eg manpower and materials, and overheating in the economy. LANSLEY's thesis is that, whilst it was only necessary to be efficient in the 1960s, it has been essential for successful companies to devote considerable resources to surveillence of environmental trends in the latter two decades. Historical analysis will not be very helpful in turbulent times; the identification and response to environmental changes is the key to success and survival in to-day's construction industry.

(c)   Structural analysis of the competitive environment
The competitive environment, partially defined in the northern hemisphere of figure 2.1, is seen as most important by businessmen

(GLUECK *et al.* 1984) and is a particular feature of the construction industry. It is the environment in which building organisations spend large amounts of resources, chiefly in the form of marketing and procuring work; it directly effects the organisation, particularly by posing threats from competitors.

To define the competitive environment it is important to understand the distinction between an industry and a market; for the strategist, this distinction can be crucial. The essential difference is that *an industry is an output concept* whilst *a market is a demand concept.* Normally, industries are defined by the Standard Industrial Classification whereby all firms supplying a particular product or service are grouped together. Whilst this may be useful for statistical purposes, it says little about competition; it merely says who supplies construction services. For the strategist, what is most important is the nature of the competition, that is, the market. Markets can be described and defined by the nature of competition. If the strategy of one company has a significant effect on the demand for the output of another firm, then it can be said that the two firms are in competition with each other and thus in the same market. In defining market boundaries it is the degree of substitutability between products or services which is the key factor. Thus, a civil engineering firm and a speculative house builder are in the same construction industry supply system but in patently different markets because a bridge is no substitute for a house and vice-versa. Equally, segments within markets can be exploited, for example the management contracting market *within* the building contracting market. This concept of markets as a basis for differentiating between firms is explained fully in FELLOWS *et al.* (1983).

Having defined a building organisation's competitive environment in terms of markets it is necessary to have a structured means of examining the competitive environment of the organisation so as to provide a clear understanding of the forces at work. A useful model for structural analysis is provided by PORTER (1980) as shown in figure 3.3.

As can be seen in the model there are five forces which create the competitive environment in which firms have to operate and thus directly threaten profitability.

(i) *Potential entrants*
The threat of new entrants is important where entry barriers to an industry or market are low. The construction industry is often cited as an example of this because 'anyone can set up as a builder' due to there being no register of builders and to the low capital requirements engendered by stage payments from the client. Whilst this may be true for small projects, eg extensions and alterations, the advent of selective competitive tendering and

management contracting means that for larger projects the barriers to entry are considerable. Experience and expertise have become essential pre-requisites for competing in these markets and the threats usually come from known competitors.

Another aspect of this is the ability of small firms to compete for large projects and, when work is scarce, the ability of large firms to compete for smaller projects. There are barriers of economies scale of operation in both cases.

(*ii*) *Substitutes*

The threat of substitute services has become more acute during the recent recession with the traditional demarcations between design and construction being reduced by design and build and management contracting. These approaches offer clients substitutes for the traditional competitive tendering methods.

In times of high interest rates, clients may see overtime working within their organisation as a substitute to extending or building a factory.

(*iii*) *Buyers*

The bargaining power of public sector clients was considerable during the period from the Second World War until the early 1970s. The power was exhibited through fierce and often cut-throat competition for work based on ridiculously large numbers of tenderers (NEWCOMBE 1978). In recent years this power has declined with the switch to private sector projects, but has led to private sector clients becoming more demanding of the industry. The ultimate example is the formation of the British Property

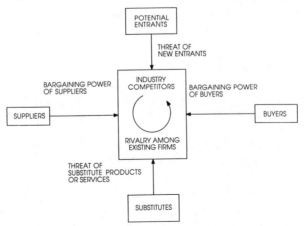

3.3   Forces driving industry competition

Federation and the development of the BPF method of conducting construction projects.

(*iv*) *Suppliers*

In an industry with low capitalisation, such as construction, the bargaining power of suppliers (and sub-contractors) is considerable. Many builders' merchants are far larger than the building firms that they supply and the withdrawal of credit has often brought bankruptcy to building contractors.

To mitigate this threat a number of larger contractors have adopted backward integration, purchasing materials suppliers, eg ready-mix concrete and plant hire companies.

(*v*) *Industry competitors*

Competitors will be concerned with the degree of rivalry between themselves *within* the construction industry. The degree of rivalry in construction markets is likely to be based on one of the following:

– the extent to which construction firms are *in balance*; balance depends on *market share* and *size* of competing firms. The construction industry is fragmented with no contractor holding a dominant position in terms of market share, although locally there may be dominant firms in a region. Even this possibility is mitigated, however, by the fact that, because of the financial structure of construction, firms of various sizes can compete on equal terms for a range of projects. The large contractor has few advantages in local markets. These factors lead to intense competition

– a market in *slow* or *fast growth* phases is likely to influence competition. As already pointed out, the construction industry in the last twenty-five years has experienced periods of slump with the resulting increase in competitiveness and periods of boom where demand exceeds supply for construction services and real competition declines

– if the addition of *extra capacity is in large increments*, as obtaining a major construction project clearly is, then the competitor winning the project may face temporary over-capacity but increase competition for the remaining firms

– if a product or service is not *differentiated* from competitors offering similar services then clients can easily switch between contractors to obtain the lowest price which again raises the degree of rivalry between them.

Each of these forces can produce opportunities as well as threats for the individual contractor depending upon how skilfully strategy is conducted. There are opportunities to agree long-term contracts with certain clients thus eliminating the competition; eg Bovis and Marks and Spencer; it is possible to differentiate the service which a firm offers, eg Bovis Management Fee contracts.

(d) Identifying the organisation's competitive position

All organisations are in a competitive position; that is, they are competing for clients and resources. This is particularly true of building contracting firms.

The competitive position of a building organisation can be identified by considering:

(*i*) *The level of demand in the market*
The construction industry is notorious for the fluctuations in demand which create feast or famine for the firms involved. As discussed earlier, there have been numerous 'booms' and 'slumps' in the industry since 1960 and obviously the competition between contractors is directly effected by the current state of the construction market. Ironically, increasing demand for the output of firms during the boom periods is usually matched by a scarcity of inputs, in the form of resources, causing overheating. The strategically sophisticated firms spot the trends and respond accordingly.

(*ii*) *The relevant competitors*
Not all firms in a particular market are competitors. *Strategic group analysis* is one means of identifying those competing organisations with similar strategic characteristics. A way of mapping a particular strategic group of competitors is given in FELLOWS *et al.* (1983) and shown in figure 3.4. This illustrates that degree of diversification of services and markets covered, and geographical decentralisation of services are two key ways of grouping construction companies. For example, Zone 1 single business companies, eg small house building firms, operating in a local area, eg Devon, are a relatively homogeneous group. These firms see each other as competitors and are, therefore, by definition, a strategic group. The same applies to Zone 4 companies who compete with each other in a number of markets and in the national and/or international construction market. There are other factors which determine the strategic grouping of firms, including size, ownership, financial gearing, quality of service and product, etc.

(*iii*) *The market leadership of the firm*
The usual source of power in a market is market share but, due to the fragmentation of the construction industry,

this is rarely achieved by construction firms. However, there are occasions on which construction companies achieve leadership through identifying and exploiting a niche. For example, McCARTHY and STONE realised that sheltered housing for a growing elderly population was a niche, which they exploited to gain leadership and thus expand and dramatically improve their profitability (GRINYER 1988). Market leadership is often temporary; competitors will attack the leader.

(e) Identifying opportunities and threats

The output of this analysis of market information will be a list of opportunities currently open to the business, together with a knowledge of the most important threats and the source of those threats. The strategic planning conversion process will take this information as inputs and convert it into strategies which exploit the opportunities and circumvent or nullify the threats.

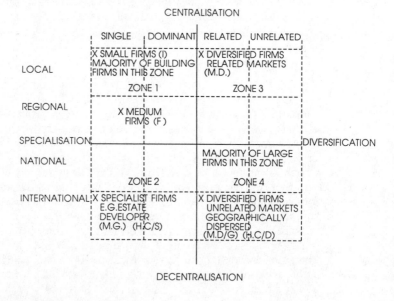

3.4   Strategy-structure model

2   Organisational forces

The analysis of external forces shaping strategic decisions which emerges from a study of market information must be complemented by an understanding of the forces *within* the firm which just as surely shape strategy.

The sources of internal organisational forces are discussed at length in FELLOWS *et al.* (1983). They are:

(a)   Corporate trading performance
(b)   Current services and products
(c)   Organisational analysis
(d)   Management succession
(e)   Employee attitude
(f)   Company position in markets
(g)   Control systems
(h)   Fixed assets
(i)   Company policy.

Typical questions which need to be answered under each of the headings outlined are:

(a)   Corporate trading performance

How do the profit levels of the company compare with competitors in the firm's 'strategic group'? During the last five years? During the last financial year?

What are the performance levels of the operating divisions within the business? Should certain unprofitable divisions be closed?

(b)   Current services and products

Which services are most profitable?

Which types of work are most profitable?

What trends are discernable in the demand for the services and types of work in which the firm specialises?

(c)   Organisational analysis

Is the firm's current organisation structure appropriate for current activities?

What are the skills and experience of the people within the business?

In what ways does the structure, skills and experience of the firm limit its choice of strategies?

This will be discussed further in chapter 3.

(d)   Management succession

Who will take over when the firm's present key personnel leave the business?

What training is being given to younger members of the firm who will have to assume responsibility?

Will replacements be sought through internal growth or
external recruitment?
See chapter 7 for a further analysis.

(e) Employee attitude
What are the career aspirations of employees?
What will be the attitude of key employees to changes which
might be created by a new strategy?
How can the firm overcome resistance to change?

(f) Company position in markets
What is the tendering success ratio of the firm?
What effect would an increase in mark up have on the
tendering success ratio?
Is the firm a market leader or a market follower?

(g) Control systems
Can the firm's information systems provide accurate, relevant
and timely information?
Should the firm's sytems be computerised?
Who takes the necessary action on the control data which is
collected?

(h) Fixed assets
How valuable is the firm's head office site? Could the firm
operate as well from a less valuable site and realise the value of
the asset?
How much own plant and equipment is fully or even
adequately utilised? Why not hire plant?

(i) Company policy
What constraints are applied to the choice of strategies by
policy decisions?
Which policies are based on the core values of the business and
which policies are now obsolete?
Can the firm afford to maintain a particular policy?

This comprehensive internal appraisal should highlight the
strengths and *weaknesses* of the company.
The findings from the searching examination of market forces
and organisational forces will enable a SWOT analysis to be made.

3 The SWOT analysis
The outcome of the analysis of the inputs to the building firm is the
building of a data base for the SWOT analysis.
The key issues from the analysis of market and organisational

appraisals can be tabulated against each other to identify areas of match and mis-match as shown in figure 3.5. A scoring system could be used with a '+' to indicate a benefit to the organisation and a '−' to show an adverse effect on the organisation. For example, high growth in the market would favour the firm's current strategy of geographical concentration, but skill shortages in the industry could lead to loss of key personnel because of low morale. A fuller analysis of 'match' is contained under *Profiles* page 65.

3.6   The conversion process

The conversion process within the strategic system is usually called the *strategy formulation* phase. It is concerned with taking the information provided by the inputs and converting it into specific

KEY MARKET FORCES	Under capacity in industry	Fragmentation	High growth in market	Ageing population	International competition	Skill shortages	Interest rates	Etc
Current strategies								
Diversification								
Geographic								
concentration			+					
Main strengths								
Owner control								
Younger members								
Reputation								
Loyal workforce								
Etc								
Main weaknesses								
management style								
Low morale						−		
Lack experience								
Risk avoidance								
Unprofitable								
divisions								
+								
TOTAL −								

3.5   *A SWOT analysis for a building contracting business*

strategies, resource allocations and structural configurations to achieve competitive advantage.

Before discussing the strategy formulation process it is important to understand the nature of strategic decisions and the ways of making such decisions. The nature of strategic decisions has already been discussed at the beginning of this chapter so that ways or modes of making decisions will be reviewed here.

Strategy making modes

MINTZBERG (1973) has identified three modes of strategic decision making – the **entrepreneurial** mode, the **adaptive** mode and the **planning** mode.

The *entrepreneurial mode* is characterised by four features:

(1) strategy making is dominated by the active search for new opportunities not on solving problems;
(2) power is centralised in the hands of the chief executive;
(3) strategy making is characterised by dramatic leaps forward in the face of uncertainty;
(4) growth is the dominant goal of the entrepreneurial organisation.

These characteristics are readily recognisable in many construction companies – even in very large construction corporations (CHANNON 1978).

Recognition of the *adaptive mode* followed the publication of two books in 1963. LINDBLOM and BRAYBROKE wrote *A Strategy of Decision* about policy making in the public sector, while CYERT and MARCH published *A Behavioral Theory of the Firm* which reviewed the realities of decision making in business organisations.

LINDBLOM's (1959) earlier description of strategic decision making as the 'science of muddling through' envisaged the decision maker as accepting a powerful status quo and the lack of clear objectives, making remedial decisions which enable him to proceed in small steps, never moving too far from the status quo.

CYERT and MARCH view the business firm as a 'shifting, multi-goal coalition' with strategists solving urgent rather than important problems and 'negotiating' objectives with groups of powerful stakeholders.

Four major characteristics distinguish the *adaptive mode*:

(1) clear goals do not exist;
(2) strategy making is characterised by 'reactive' solutions to existing problems rather than the 'proactive' search for new opportunities;
(3) the adaptive organisation makes its decisions in incremental serial steps;

(4)   disjointed and inconsistent decisions are characteristic of the adaptive organisation.

Much of the strategic planning literature (ANSOFF 1965, ANDREWS 1980, ARGENTI 1980) only recognised the *planning mode.* What is usually called strategic or corporate planning is synonymous with the planning mode. There are three essential features of the *planning mode*:

(1)   the analyst plays a major role in strategy making. The separation of analysis from decision making is the result. The planning analysts conduct in-depth studies of issues and propose optional strategies to the strategists who make the decisions;

(2)   the planning mode focuses on systematic analysis, particularly in the assessment of the costs and benefits of competing proposals. In contrast to the entrepreneurial and adaptive modes, it involves a systematic and structured search for new opportunities as well as the solution of existing problems;

(3)   the integration of decisions and strategies is a key feature. Decisions made together in a systematic process are less likely to conflict and more likely to complement each other than if they were made independently. The results are global strategies which provide strategic direction for the whole organisation. A recent study by AWAD (1988) indicates that this is the approach adopted by a majority of large construction companies.

Smaller building firms facing simple and/or single markets may find the entrepreneurial or adaptive modes perfectly adequate. As firms expand and diversify the complexities they face demand a more systematic and less intuitive method of strategy making; a method that employs specialist staff to develop parallel rather than sequential opportunities by a continuous *proactive* process rather forcing the firm into a *reactive* posture.

Strategy formulation is not as neat as some of the text books might suggest and inevitably involves an element of 'muddling through'. In an article entitled 'Systematic Strategic Planning for Construction Firms', GRINYER (1972) proposes a model which incorporates the features of the planning mode, but allows the strategic decision makers considerable flexibility to reiterate earlier steps in the process. As GRINYER points out:

'It is clear that any systematic approach to the formulation of strategies should allow for the dynamic, continuous nature of the process. Actual and anticipated performance of the firm in a changing market environment, in which fortunes are strongly affected by economic trends, central and local government policies, and the behaviour of competitors, need to be regularly monitored as part of the approach.

'Likewise, it should lead to a regular review of the strategies by which the board will seek to attain its objectives, by means of parallel search and evaluation of opportunities in the light of the strengths and weaknesses of the firm, potential for realising the objectives in various markets and actual and expected competitive forces.'

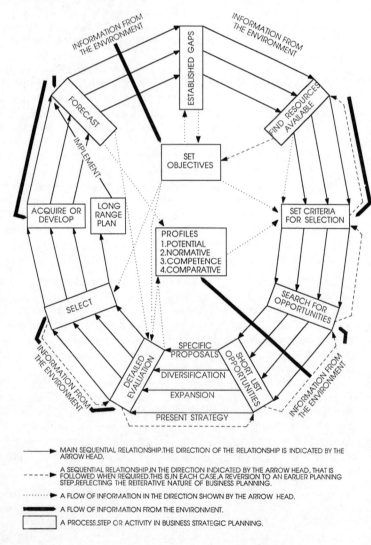

3.6   A conceptual model of business strategic planning

The model with GRINYER proposed is shown in figure 3.6 and the rest of this section is based on an exposition of this model.

A model of the strategic conversion process
The model comprises twelve strategic activities which are of two types. Some of these activities – set objectives, set criteria for selection, select, acquire or buy – require *decisions*. These are the activities which must be done by strategic managers. The other activities are *analytical* in nature, data must be processed from both the inputs and outputs of the strategic system to provide a basis for decision making.

The twelve activities are linked by four types of flow:

(1) *Main sequential flow* – this shows the normal chronological sequence of activities.

(2) *Optional sequential flow* – this may be followed when required. This flow permits a reversion to an earlier strategic activity and allows reiteration of steps in the process, especially the development from present strategy to expansion, diversification and specific proposals.

(3) *Information flows* – there are flows of information in addition to the sequential flows; for example, objectives are a central source of information in setting criteria, detailed evaluation and selection. Detailed evaluation also requires information from forecasts and profiles.

(4) *Environmental information flows* – these flows stress the essentially interactive nature of the strategic system and its context. From figure 1.3 it can be seen that the strategic system is linked to the other organisational systems and to the external environment. Strategic decisions are so significant that they will affect all these other systems, the reactions from which will provide feedback to the strategists on the success or otherwise of their strategies.

The operation of the model commences with the emergence of a *gap* between the expected performance and the objectives. This gap may appear because *forecast* performance has to be revised downwards due to market conditions. For instance, the recent (1988) increase in interest rates has put a brake on the boom in the construction industry and will depress the expected performance of many building organisations. Equally a gap may be created by an upward revision of *objectives*. Both forecasts and objectives are related to the stage in the boom-slump cycle at which they are set. At the start of the boom they may be too modest; a drop in demand may reveal them as too ambitious.

Once a gap has been established then the cycle of activities shown in figure 3.5 will occur as strategic management seek to narrow or eliminate the gap between performance and objectives. Typically, the process will follow the outer ring of the main sequential flow first which entails focusing on the *existing strategies*. The gap may be closed by the more efficient operation of the firm, thus reducing operating and overhead costs, or by more effective penetration of the firm's existing markets through improved tender success ratios or better marketing to clients and architects.

Only when the potential to achieve the objectives through existing strategies has been exhausted will firms normally consider *expansion* into related markets; and only when expansion has failed to close the gap will *diversification* into unrelated markets be attractive. The sequence of existing to expansion to diversification strategies is typical because of the increasing risk and uncertainty encountered when a firm moves out of its existing and familiar markets. The sequence was first profiled by ANSOFF (1965) in terms of a product/market matrix (see figure 3.9). This matrix is adapted by GRINYER to the construction industry and shown in figure 3.7.

Whether existing, expansion or diversification strategies are chosen the basic process shown in the model (figure 3.5) is followed:

Objectives are set by the strategic decision makers, a *forecast* is made of the extent to which current strategies will achieve the objectives and the size and nature of the *gap* identified. Examination of the *competence profile* and the *resources available* will reveal the strengths and weaknesses of the firm which in conjunction with the objectives will enable the strategists to establish the *criteria for selection*. These criteria guide the identification of general areas in which to *search for opportunities* and the *short listing* of favoured opportunities worth *detailed evaluation*. The evaluation may require the construction of *potential*, *normative*, *competence* and *comparative profiles* as an aid to the analysis of opportunities in terms of their potential to meet the objectives, the strengths and skills required to exploit an opportunity and the extent to which the firm possesses the necessary competence. Profiles for each opportunity will be needed.

From this analysis a set of preferred options can be presented to strategic management who will *select* a strategy, eg geographic expansion of existing services, and a mode of achieving the strategy, eg *acquire* an existing firm in the area chosen or *develop* the firm's own assets by opening a regional office. These decisions will be written into the *long range plan* which is the planning document which provides the basis for implementing strategies and controlling their progress.

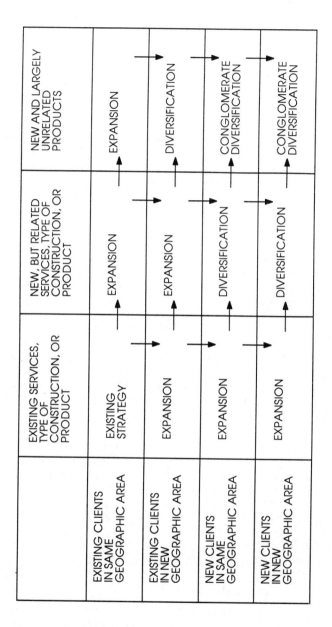

	EXISTING SERVICES, TYPE OF CONSTRUCTION, OR PRODUCT	NEW, BUT RELATED SERVICES, TYPE OF CONSTRUCTION, OR PRODUCT	NEW AND LARGELY UNRELATED PRODUCTS
EXISTING CLIENTS IN SAME GEOGRAPHIC AREA	EXISTING STRATEGY	→ EXPANSION	→ EXPANSION
EXISTING CLIENTS IN NEW GEOGRAPHIC AREA	→ EXPANSION	→ EXPANSION	→ DIVERSIFICATION
NEW CLIENTS IN SAME GEOGRAPHIC AREA	→ EXPANSION	→ DIVERSIFICATION	→ CONGLOMERATE DIVERSIFICATION
NEW CLIENTS IN NEW GEOGRAPHIC AREA	→ EXPANSION	→ DIVERSIFICATION	→ CONGLOMERATE DIVERSIFICATION

3.7   Alternative strategies

The forecast of the extent to which the proposed strategies will meet the objectives of the firm re-activates the process if necessary.

Deviations from the process are almost inevitable because of changing circumstances and the optional sequential flows allow for this.

Having outlined the strategic conversion process, a more detailed examination of the activities will now be made.

Set objectives

Objectives, once set, are not fixed, but will continuously change over time in response to internal and external forces. Potential and actual performance of selected strategies may necessitate the revision upwards or downwards of objectives. Equally, objectives are the basis for measuring performance. For example, a building company may set profit targets to be achieved by its speculative housing division in a particular year. This profit target will provide a benchmark against which to measure the performance of the division. If progress reporting reveals that the division will not meet its target due to external forces, eg change in interest rates depressing demand, or internal forces, eg inefficient site management, then strategic management will have to revise the profit target downwards. This may entail seeking higher profits from other business activities to maintain corporate profit levels.

As indicated earlier in this chapter when discussing the adaptive mode, firms do not have a single objective, but rather, multiple objectives, which may be inconsistent or actually conflict. This arises from the nature of the coalition of stakeholders who often represent conflicting objectives.

The objectives may be expressed in quantitative or qualitative terms. The precision of quantified objectives is preferred for effective measurement of performance, whilst accepting that some important objectives cannot be quantified.

Two types of objectives are evident in most organisations – *economic* and *non-economic*. Economic objectives can usually be quantified whereas non-economic objectives are more likely to be qualitative.

GRINYER identifies typical economic and non-economic objectives for construction companies.

ECONOMIC OBJECTIVES

General competitve strength
(i)   Growth of turnover, earnings, market share in existing markets and number of markets in which the firm operates (types of construction, clients, localities, etc).

(ii)   Stability of annual gross turnover, gross profit, ratio of gross profit to total assets, fixed assets or shareholders' equity, and in utilisation of scarce physical or human resources held by the firm.

Internal efficiency of the firm
  (i)   Gross margin on total annual value of work completed: annual turnover of net worth, fixed capital or current assets: annual turnover on other critical and scarce resources valued at market prices.
  (ii) Depth of management, technical or operative skills.
  (iii) Age of plant or unsold speculative building.
  (iv) Effectiveness of the organisational structure, administrative and operating systems and management information systems.

Flexibility or the sensitivity of performance to unforeseen contingencies:
  (i)   Offensive external flexibility: the existence of the necessary base of technological skills and management experience to seize new opportunities.
  (ii) Defensive external flexibility: operation within a sufficiently large number of localities on a sufficiently wide range of types of structures, and with a sufficiently large number and set of types of ultimate client to minimise the effects of adverse, major changes in the market.
  (iii) Internal strength to meet major set-backs and take advantage of opportunities: financial strength as measured by the ratios of current assets to current liabilities, cash and debtors to current liabilities, current assets to fixed assets, and equity of the shareholders (net worth) to total debt: resources, organisational structure and operating, administrative and management information systems to allow rapid response to new challenges or opportunities.

NON-ECONOMIC
(a)   Internal political, eg retention of control by the existing owners or board.
(b)   External political, eg to avoid intervention by central, local or other governmental bodies.
(c)   To meet reasonable aspirations of employees and to develop them to their full potential.
(d)   To serve clients and the general community well.
(e)   To maintain a good reputation within the industry.

A successful and stable firm may be able to pursue both kinds of objectives, but when a firm is fighting for survival, economic objectives will over-ride other considerations.

Find resources available

The auditing of resources to determine availability and utilisation of resources has been discussed under inputs. This, together with the competence profile of the business, will enable an assessment to be made of the strengths and weaknesses of the firm. To facilitate a comparison with the objectives it may be helpful to classify the strengths and weaknesses under the same headings as the objectives. Particular consideration will have to be given to facilities and equipment, employees' skills, organisational experience and the abilities of general and operational managers. A shortfall in available resources may force a re-think about objectives.

Criteria for selection

From the objectives and the analysis of the strengths and weaknesses of the firm will emerge the criteria for selecting areas for the opportunity search and for the filtering out of unattractive options during the short-listing and selection phases of the process. Again, it may be helpful to set criteria in the same terms as the objectives in order to identify opportunities which are more likely to achieve the aims of the strategy makers. Typical criteria in selecting a market might be growth potential, return on investment, profitability, ease of entry and exit, as well as non-economic aspirations such as enhancing the firm's reputation or providing for the personal development of employees.

Search for opportunities

A selective search for opportunities is likely to begin, for a building contractor, with a study of the building and civil engineering market. Within this market, segments can be classified by type of client or end-user, type of construction skills required, geographical locations, payment methods, competition, likely profit levels, procurement methods, etc. The search should try to find a niche within a market for the firm. For example, McCarthy and Stone have successfully specialised in sheltered housing and nursing homes for the elderly since the mid-seventies, a niche over-looked by the larger house builders such as Barrett and Wimpey. In fact, the recognition of the opportunity offered by the 'elderly' market is considered to be a prime factor in the survival of the company following the 1974 slump in the building industry (Grinyer 1988). Following the exploration of existing market segments, attention may be focused on related markets, where common skills and support services can be exploited to achieve synergistic advantages. A company may know that it excels in undertaking work with a high degree of repetition and, therefore, in reviewing different markets will seek opportunities that utilise this skill, eg housing – public and private, factory units, multi-storey office blocks, etc.

A systematic procedure for conducting an opportunity search has been suggested by De Bono (1978).

Short list opportunities
Short-listing involves rejecting the majority of opportunities
because they do not meet the criteria established at the start of the
search. This is an important activity primarily because of the time
and expense involved in the next activity, detailed evaluation. The
foundation of any successful strategy is the elimination of 'losers'
and the spotting of 'winners' through the progressive filtering
process described. Inevitably, short-listing will eliminate some
'winners' and retain some 'losers' because of the limitations
imposed by imperfect knowledge, poor judgment and the sheer
uncertainty of the construction industry. The consolation is that the
planning mode described here is likely to produce consistently more
winners than either the entrepreneurial or adaptive modes of
strategy formulation.

Detailed evaluation
Two methods of detailed evaluation of opportunities are shown in
the model.

The first involves the detailed examination of short-listed opportunities by reference to the stated objectives of the firm. Again the list
of objectives would prove a useful framework for evaluation.
Economic evaluation would consider the potential growth of markets
and segments, the opportunities for increasing turnover in particular
markets given the costs of entry, the strength of competition and the
probable market share, and the gross margins likely to be achieved on
different types of contract for different types of client in different
locations. The effect on profits of payment methods, funding required,
and size of contract are other factors which should also be taken into
account. Non-economic factors may be the utilisation of spare
capacity – plant, design, management – and the creation of synergy in
marketing or production. The stability provided by a market to offset
the fluctuations in other markets may be important, for instance
repairs and maintenance or public sector contracts may balance more
speculative ventures. The extent to which an opportunity exploits the
identified strengths of the company and meets other non-economic
objectives and constraints will also be a key consideration.

Profiles
The second method of detailed evaluation requires the construction
of profiles; the process is described by GRINYER as follows:

> Use of potential, normative, competence and comparative
> profiles in detailed evaluation of specific opportunities is illus-
> trated in figure 3.8. Clearly the potential profile indicates the
> contribution that the opportunity could make to attainment of
> the objectives of the firm, in terms of growth, stability, internal
> efficiency and internal and external flexibility. As already stated,

the normative profile states the organisational, management, operational, marketing and financial strengths necessary fully to realise this potential together with the necessary physical resources.

Comparison of the normative and competence profiles leads to

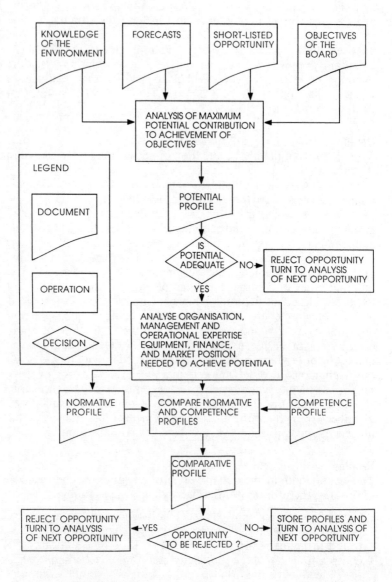

3.8   Use of profiles

a statement of the extent to which the firm has what it takes to achieve the full potential, and any aspects in which it is not currently fitted to do so. It is clear that the normative, competence and comparative profiles must be expressed in the same terms to permit comparison, and the same basic format is useful in this respect.

Select
This is the fundamental strategic decision making activity. At this point in the process the analysis has thrown up a number of well researched options and a choice must be made. The strategists may choose to accept any or all of the options or may decide to reject all the options proposed. The evident advantage of the planning mode over the other two modes becomes apparent at this stage. The parallel search will have produced a set of opportunities rather than the single opportunity which emerges from the sequential search pattern. The option proposed will probably offer a balance between high risk – high profit ventures, eg property development, and low risk – modestly profitable work, such as local authority contracts. In making the decisions the strategy makers will refer to stated objectives and criteria together with an assessment of the quality of the forecasts made in the proposals.

The long range plan
Once proposals have been selected they are written into the strategic plan of the company. This document, the nature and content of which is described in detail in FELLOWS *et al.* (1983), will provide the basis for communication, implementation and control.

Acquire or develop
In parallel with the commitment to particular strategies recorded in the long range plan will be further strategic decisions about whether it is possible or desirable to achieve these strategies by internal growth or through acquisition of appropriate businesses. A study by CHANNON (1978) of large construction companies revealed that the longer established companies in the sample (Laing, Wimpey, Taylor-Woodrow and Costain) had mainly grown through an internal development, 'home-grown' policy. The new companies (Trafalgar House, London and Northern) had used acquisition as the main vehicle for achieving their spectacular growth.

The overriding factor in the decision appears to be the rate of growth that the company wants to attain, but other aspects are the desire of the owners to retain control of the firm, the financial strength of the business, the problems of entry into a new market (buying-in may be easier than developing), the availability of suitable candidates for take-over or merger, spare capacity that the firm has, etc. Two other methods which are popular in the construction industry are *joint ventures* and *licences or agencies*. The first has the advantage of pooling experience and risk whilst reducing capital requirements: the second approach avoids the often substantial costs of developing a product or service and the ability to offer quickly a tried and tested facility to clients.

Joint ventures are often a feature of overseas projects where the other partner is frequently an indigenous contractor. This eases entry into the market. Licences and agencies are frequently used for prefabricated buildings or specialised services such as drain clearance.

Forecasting and establishing gaps
GRINYER (1972) says:

> The objective of forecasts is to provide a basis for strategic decisions by indicating the extent to which existing strategy, possible expansion strategies and possible diversification strategies, are likely to contribute to achievement of the objectives of the board.
>
> Thus it is intimately linked with *gap analysis*, the gap being nothing but a residual: the difference between forecast performance and the objectives. Each time a decision is made to extend the strategy, this gap may be further closed, and may indeed become negative.

As stated earlier, the forecast of the extent to which the proposed strategies will meet the objectives of the firm re-activates the process if necessary.

Conclusion

The approach to strategy formulation outlined in the model in figure 3.6 offers the advantages of a full, rational and continuous process with the flexibility of reviewing and reiterating earlier phases if necessary. It also allows firms to move incrementally through existing to expansion to diversification strategies.

The parallel search for opportunities will generate many more well researched options for strategic management than other approaches which should lead to improved quality in decision making. Communications within the firm should improve because of the explicit statement of objectives and strategies; this in turn should contribute to creation of the elusive corporate harmony which has been shown to be a feature of high performing companies (PETERS and WATERMAN 1982, GOLDSMITH and CLUTTERBUCK 1984).

The cyclical nature of the process suggested by the model stresses the continuous surveillance of the environment which should ensure that fewer opportunities are missed or threats overlooked.

There are, however, certain conditions which need to exist in the business if the systematic approach is to work effectively. The top management of the firm must be committed to the approach and be seen to be enthusiastic. The establishment of a strategy team which involves key functional managers as well as general managers is essential. Certain members of the team can be full time in the larger company, but the important aspect again is that a team is created which is committed to the strategy concept and process (ARGENTI 1980).

Lastly, it is crucial that the firm has the necessary management information systems (see chapter 5) to effectively monitor and control the inputs and the implementation of strategy.

3.7 Outputs

The outputs of the strategic system are decisions – *strategic, administrative and operational* as shown in figure 3.1 – designed to meet the objectives of the stakeholders in the business and to achieve *competitive advantage.*

Strategic decisions
ANSOFF (1965) says that 'Strategic decisions are primarily concerned with external rather than internal problems' and specifically with the selection of the services which the firm will offer and the markets in which it will operate.

The outcome of strategic decisions are strategies. Strategies may be classified in a number of ways. Three classification schemes are given here and their applications to the building organisation discussed. The three schemes arise from three schools of thought about strategy:

1 The Growth Vector school
2 The Strategy-Structure school
3 The Competitive Advantage school.

1 The Growth Vector school
This approach to the delineation of strategies was discussed in the conversion process section and forms an integral part of the model shown in figure 3.6

ANSOFF's (1965) original product/market matrix (shown in figure 3.9) generated four 'growth vectors' of *market penetration, market development, product (or service) development* and *diversification.* Market penetration and product (or service) development are strategies adopted within the firm's existing market, whilst market development and diversification will direct the firm into new markets.

CARLISLE (1987) studied the extent to which fifteen Northern Ireland contractors and five UK contractors had adopted ANSOFF's 'growth vector' strategies. The strategies were firstly related to the objectives of the firms in terms of *growth* in turnover with acceptable levels of profit, *stasis*, ie maintaining the current turnover in real terms, with, if possible, increasing levels of profit and '*survival*'.

The five firms with a growth objective had attempted to enter new geographical markets and all but one had also diversified into new products and new markets.

The one firm aiming for stasis had adopted a market development strategy and those contractors merely attempting to survive 'strongly favoured product development as a means of doing so'.

When the strategies were correlated with performance, the results showed that '. . . more of the top performers than of the average or poor performers had tried a new external strategy'. No single strategy was more successful than the others, but it was concluded that '. . . the actual strategy adopted may be of less importance than the fact of having a strategy and implementing it'.

An expansion by GRINYER (1972) of ANSOFF's strategies is shown in figure 3.7. This model is particularly useful for construction firms.

2 The Strategy-Structure school

This school of strategic thought originated in the research and

PRODUCTS

	EXISTING	NEW
EXISTING (MARKETS)	MARKET PENETRATION	PRODUCT DEVELOPMENT
NEW (MARKETS)	MARKET DEVELOPMENT	DIVERSIFICATION

3.9 Growth vectors

writings of CHANDLER (1966), who traced the organisational histories of four major American corporations. He defined strategy in terms of the degree of diversification and geographic expansion adopted by the business. The extent of diversification and geographic expansion were found to have implications for organisational design and performance. This led CHANDLER to the proposition that 'structure follows strategy' in successful firms.

Chandler's pioneering work was refined by CHANNON (1978) and applied to the service industries in the UK: the sample included seven construction corporations – Richard Costain, Taylor-Woodrow, John Laing, George Wimpey, Trafalgar House, Wood Hall Trust and London Northern Securities.

The classification of strategies developed by CHANNON is shown in figure 3.10. This classification suggests that an organisation's strategy has three major dimensions:

(a) Diversification

Most firms start in the *Single Business* category, eg house building. Costain, Taylor-Woodrow, Laing and Wimpey started in this way. Many construction firms choose to remain in this category if they can obtain enough work of the chosen type. This would then become the existing strategy of the firm, shown in figure 3.6.

Expansion strategies can be of two types. The *Dominant Business* strategy involves staying within a single market but adding peripheral activities. For example, a general contractor whose work load is dominated by competitive tendering, may build a small number of speculative houses for sale if the opportunity arises. The alternative strategy is to move into *Related Business*. There is now no dominant type of work but rather a number of related activities which represent a balanced portfolio of interests. Typically a construction firm might have interests in building, civil engineering, house building, building products, site investigation and so on. The Related Business strategy spreads the risk over a range of activities;

Diversification

Single business	Firms which grew by the expansion of one business activity so that at least 95 per cent of sales lay within this single business area.
Dominant business	Firms which grew primarily by the expansion of one main product line but which in addition had added other business activities making up 30 per cent or less of the total sales or its equivalent. These secondary activities might be related to the primary activity as for example with the petro-chemical interests of an oil company or unrelated as say the cosmetics interests of a tobacco company.

Continued. . .

Continued. . .
Related businesses

Firms which grew by expansion by means of entry into related markets by the use of related technology, by related vertical activities or some combinations of these strategies such that no one business area accounted for 70 per cent of the total corporate sales or its equivalent.

Unrelated businesses

Firms which grew by expansion (usually by acquisition) into new markets and new technologies unrelated to the firm's original business so that no one business area accounted for 70 per cent of total corporate sales or its equivalent.

International activities

High international activity

Where 40 per cent or more of corporate sales were generated from international operations.

Medium international activity

Where more than 10 per cent but less than 40 per cent of corporate sales (or equivalent) were generated from international operations.

Low international activity

Where 10 per cent or less of corporate sales were generated from international operations.

Acquisitions type

Horizontal (H)

The extension of the same range of products or services to the same basic customer group.

Integrated (I)

The extension of a business by forward integration toward the market place or backward to sources of supply.

Related (R)

Diversification either by the addition of related products selling to an established customer group or by the extension of the existing services to new customer groups.

Conglomerate (C)

The addition of new businesses to service markets which have no relationship to the firm's existing activities.

Acquisition rate

Aggressive acquirers

Where the number of acquisitions undertaken in the decade from 1964–74 was 10 or more.

Moderate acquirers

Where the number of acquisitions undertaken in the decade from 1964–74 was more than 3 but less than 10.

Passive acquirers

Where the number of acquisitions undertaken in the decade from 1964–74 was 3 or less.

3.10   Strategic variables

if a Single or Dominant Business strategy fails the company could be in jeopardy. Contractors who specialised in public sector work ran into difficulties during the 1970s with the political climate favouring private, rather than public, spending.

Diversification strategies into *Unrelated Businesses* are equally risky. Firms adopting this strategy are into the unknown territory at the bottom right-hand corner of figure 3.7. An example of a construction company who has successfully pursued this strategy is Trafalgar House whose interests are as diverse as property, construction, newspapers and shipping.

(*b*) *International activity*
Many construction firms have chosen to expand outside the UK in order to achieve growth targets or to offset fluctuations in their home market. The level of international activity is a matter of strategic choice for the company, bearing in mind the risks and potential profits of overseas projects. Risks may be mitigated by a joint venture with an indigenous contractor as discussed earlier.

(*c*) As discussed under the conversion process, the *type* and *rate* of acquisition are crucial strategic decisions which are largely determined by the rate of growth to which the firm aspires. CHANNON'S (1978) study revealed that the more recently formed construction corporations, Trafalgar House, Wood Hall Trust and London and Northern had achieved their impressive size by a strategy of aggressive acquisition. The longer established companies in the sample had generally elected for a strategy of internal development as the vehicle for expansion and diversification.

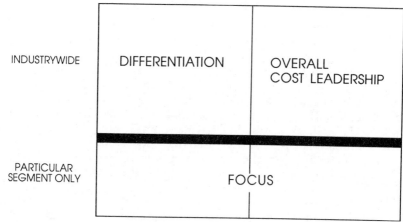

3.11   *Three generic strategies*

3　The Competitive Advantage school

PORTER (1980) states that the primary objective of the business firm is to obtain and sustain *competitive advantage* over other firms in the industry. That is, that the firm exhibits some form of distinctive competence by which customers or clients can distinguish its products or services.

PORTER asserts that there are three *generic* strategies which businesses can pursue in order to achieve competitive advantage. The three generic strategies are illustrated in figure 3.11.

1　Cost leadership

Adoption of this strategy means that a company seeks to offer consistently lower prices than its competitors to a broad range of clients, as a means of securing work.

This strategy is particularly relevant in the construction industry where a majority of work is let by competitive tender, usually to the lowest bidder. In open tendering the competition is solely on price and in selective tendering the pre-selection of contractors on criteria other than price means that ultimately selection is on the basis of price. The attempt by a construction company to obtain cost leadership through lower prices may be a temporary strategy when the firm's workload is low or in response to a recession in the industry.

The source of cost leadership derives mainly from synergy in operations or marketing. For example, backward integration by a contractor who purchases a ready mix concrete company may enable the firm to quote lower prices for concrete work due to its access to low cost sources of raw materials. Equally a contractor who has computer-based systems for handling repetitive construction work, eg speculative housing, may be more competitive in public sector housing where similar control systems can be used.

2　Differentiation

The second type of generic strategy is that of *differentiation* of the organisation's strategies from that of major competitors. This means that the building organisation must offer a service which is seen by construction clients to be distinctive. This is difficult to achieve under competitive tendering, but is possible if a company is prepared to adopt other approaches to obtaining work. The Management Fee method was pioneered by Bovis to enable them to differentiate their service from that of competitors.

Quality of work and the use of directly employed craftsmen is promoted by some builders as a distinctive service to clients.

3　Focus

The two previous generic strategies are for industry wide application, but a firm may decide to *focus* on a particular segment of the market. For example, aiming at a particular type of client, as McCarthy and Stone have done so successfully, or concentrating on a small geographic area, are focus strategies.

The study by Carlisle (1987) also covered the use of the three generic strategies by the fifteen Northern Ireland building contractors and the five UK contractors. It was revealed that, of the twenty companies in the sample, twelve had adopted the cost leadership strategy, seven had pursued a strategy of focus and only one company had attempted to differentiate its services. When the performance of the three strategies was compared, cost leadership was found to be less successful than focus, although there was no proven link between a particular strategy and success. Again, the importance of having a strategy seems to be more important that the particular strategy adopted.

The remaining two classes of decisions – administrative and operating – are mainly concerned with the *implementation* of strategy.

Administrative decisions

Ansoff defines administrative decisions as 'concerned with structuring the firms resources in a way which creates a maximum performance potential'.

There are three types of administrative decision:

(a) *Organisation*: the structure of information, authority and responsibility flows. This will be covered in chapter 4 and chapter 5.

(b) *Structure of resource conversion*: work flows, distribution system, facilities location. This will be dealt with in chapter 6.

(c) *Resource utilisation and development*: financing, facilities and equipment, personnel, materials. This will be explained in Volume 2 chapters 2, 3, 4 and 5.

Operating decisions

Ansoff contends that operating decisions '. . . usually absorb the bulk of the firms energy and attention'. The object is to maximise the efficiency of the resource conversion process . . . or, in this context, the construction production process.

Decisions are required in the following areas:
Operating objectives and goals; these are referred to in chapter 6.
Pricing and output levels are covered in chapter 5.
Marketing policies and strategy for building firms are explained in chapter 7.
Operating levels, scheduling, programming, control, etc, are briefly covered in chapter 6. For fuller information reference should be

made to Burgess and White (1979), Calvert (1981), or Oxley and
Poskitt (1980).

These three classes of decisions are interdependent. Strategic
decisions of the types discussed earlier impose operating
requirements which must be worked out at the business
(administrative) and project levels. For example, the strategic
decision of a general contractor to diversify into speculative house
building creates operating problems of pricing and marketing the
houses and the special problems of managing repetitive production.
It also triggers administrative decisions about setting up an
organisation structure for the new venture, (perhaps a 'homes'
division), the recruiting of personnel skilled in this type of work, the
raising of finance and decisions about land acquisition.

3.8   Strategic control

Figure 3.1 indicated a feedback loop from Competitive Advantage
in the form of *strategic control*. The basis for control is the Long
Range Plans of the firm as mentioned earlier. These plans together
with the resulting forecasts, enable the business to judge its ongoing
performance. When gaps appear between expected and actual
performance the strategic control system will recognise the gaps,
assess whether the variations from the plan are acceptable or not,
and alert the strategic managers who are operating the cycle of
activities shown in figure 3.6.

3.9   Summary

The role of the strategic system in the survival and success of the
building contracting firm cannot be over estimated.

As has been shown, the system receives inputs from external and
internal sources and relies heavily on information from the other
systems of the organisation shown in figure 1.3.

The implementation of strategies, which is the output of the
strategic system also depends upon these other organisational
systems. The process of strategy formulation, the conversion
process, has been explained as a cyclical process. The formality with
which the strategy process is carried out will depend on the strategy
making mode adopted by the firm's strategic managers.

Questions

1   Examine the extent to which a company's corporate objectives
    concerning profit can complement those relating to social
    responsibility.   CIOB *Building Management I* 1986

2 Formulation, documentation and implementation are stages in
   the corporate planning process.
   Detail each of these stages as they might apply to corporate
   planning in a building company.

   CIOB *Building Management II* 1986

3 Identify the sectors into which the building market can be
   divided and discuss the methods of work procurement for each.

   CIOB *Building Management II* 1987

4 Analyse the means by which a building company might ensure
   that policies determined by the Board of Directors are imple-
   mented at site level.

   CIOB *Building Management II* 1988

4 The Organisation System

A primary output of the Strategic System as outlined in chapter 3 is *administrative decisions*. These decisions determine the formal structure of the organisation. The structure of an organisation comprises all the arrangements by which its various activities are divided up between its members and their efforts co-ordinated. Typical structural decisions to be made are:

- the allocation of tasks and responsibilities to individuals
- who is to report to whom
- how authority is to be delegated
- how the organisation's activities are to be shared between departments or divisions
- how to integrate the efforts of different groups.

There are clearly different solutions to these decisions for each organisation and this will create different organisation structures. This is the essence of the modern *contingency* view of organisations which suggests that to operate efficiently an organisation needs an *appropriate* structure. The structure that is best for one organisation may not suit another and what is best now may not be right next year.

So far we have been focusing on the *authority structure* of the organisation which can be captured in an organisation chart or organigram. This was the main interest of the early management writers such as WEBER (1947) and FAYOL (1949). The concept of clear authority structures and efficient 'machine-like' operation was a product of this era. A reaction to this 'machine theory' of organisation was spearheaded by MAYO (1945) in the famous Hawthorn experiment. This work and subsequent research by McGREGOR (1960), LIKERT (1967) and ARGYRIS (1957) recognised that a *social structure* existed alongside the formal authority structure. This social structure is sometimes called the *informal organisation*.

More recent research has concentrated on the *power structure* of organisations [CYERT and MARCH (1963), MINTZBERG (1983) and KAKABADSE (1987)]. This work has attempted to understand the way in which power is wielded within organisations. The authority structure may emerge by accident or be designed by the managers of the organisation. The social and power structures evolve in response to individual needs.

4.1 A model of the organisation system

The authority, social and power structures are the *outputs* of the organisation system as shown in figure 4.1.

The *inputs* to the organisation system in figure 4.1 are sets of variables which has been found to influence organisational decisions, age and size, operations, environment and stakeholders.

Three interlocking and interdependent conversion processes occur within the organisation to create the three structures – a *structural process*, a *social process* and a *power process*.

If the input – conversion – output process is working properly then the result will be the *effective operation* of the organisation. This stresses the role of the organisation system which is to facilitate operational performance – it is a means to the end of achieving the stakeholders' objectives and strategies and should never become an end in itself.

However, problems will inevitably arise and a key part of the feedback mechanism is to be able to recognise the *symptoms* of mal-organisation as illustrated in figure 4.1.

4.2 Primary task

The Primary Task of the organisation system is:
To divide up and co-ordinate the work of the organisation to achieve operational performance.

This definition stresses the importance of the authority structure whilst allowing for the constraints applied by the social and power structures of the organisation.

4.3 Inputs

There are four sets of variables shown in figure 4.1 which have been found to effect the structuring of organisations. These are the *inputs* which are fed into the conversion process to create a unique organisation system.

Whilst for purposes of analysis these variables are treated separately, in practice they overlap and interact.

Age and size
Three effects of **age** on structure have been noted.

1   The older the organisation the more formalised is its behaviour. Young organisations do not have the precedents, policies or procedures which emerge as organisations mature. As firms age they experience events which repeat themselves so they devise

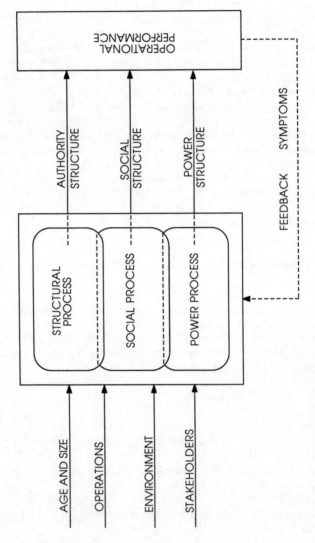

4.1   A systems model of the Organisation System

decision rules or 'programmed decisions' (SIMON 1960) to deal with these recurring events. A mature building company will have procedures for purchasing materials, hiring plant, obtaining quotations, as well as policies in respect of safety, welfare, subcontractors, supporting research, etc.

2 Older organisations have a tendency to be more decentralised and to have more autonomy (PUGH *et al.* 1969). As the organisation out-lives the founder it is likely that power will become more widely distributed to family members or shareholders with a consequent increase in autonomy. The histories of construction firms well illustrate this principle.

3 The structure of the firm reflects the age of founding of the industry. This aspect of age derives from the research of STINCHCOMBE (1965), who related the structure of building organisations to the pre-factory origin of the construction industry. Such organisations would, according to STINCHCOMBE, exhibit a *craft* structure with little bureaucracy and reliance on unpaid family workers and self-employed owners. These features seem to be typical of many small and medium sized contractors and are a reflection of the long established characteristics of the construction industry. Increasing size, however, tends to mitigate this influence.

There is overwhelming evidence from research (KHANDWALLA 1977; BLAU *et al.* 1976; PUGH *et al* 1968) for a link between increased **size** and the elaboration of structure, ie greater specialisation and differentiation of its units, together with a more developed administrative component. In short, the larger the organisation, the more bureaucratic its structure and the greater the need for sophisticated co-ordinating devices to ensure the integration of activities. The implications of this for organisational design will be worked out in the conversion process section.

It is clear that large construction corporations do exhibit many of the features of bureaucracy – specialisation, formalisation, a clear hierarchy, promotion by merit, impersonal rewards and sanctions, etc.

As a consequence of greater specialisation, differentiation and the standardisation of routines in larger organisations the size of units is larger with managers having wider spans of control. The chief estimator in a large contracting firm with computerised estimating techniques can supervise many more staff than the estimator in the smaller contractor with less sophisticated systems.

A further result of increased size is greater formalisation (PUGH 1968) with resort to rules, procedures, job descriptions, formal communications, and similar devices aimed at formalising behaviour.

The combined effects of age and size on organisations have been explored by GREINER (1972), CHANNON (1978) and WEINSHALL

(1971). Both GREINER and CHANNON were able to identify phases in the growth of large corporations which were characterised by gradual change or *evolution* interspersed with periods of rapid change or *revolution*.

GREINER argues that the seeds of destruction of the current organisational configuration are sown during its own lifetime by the nature of the phase of development. For example the *creativity* phase following the founding of the organisation by an entrepreneur leads to a *crisis of leadership* because the entrepreneur leaves the firm or loses control because of increasing size. If the leadership problem is solved by the introduction of professional managers and tighter controls, leading to the greater *direction* of activities, this, in turn may stifle initiative so that members of the organisation seek greater autonomy, thus precipitating the next crisis.

CHANNON (1978) also describes this process as shown in figure 4.2:

> The process of strategic and structural change observed among the service industry corporations does not seem to be a smooth evolutionary process. Rather change tends to take place in relatively sharp discontinuities. These are followed by periods of consolidation when the new pattern adopted as an outcome of the period of turbulence gradually evolves until a new turbulent phase ensues.

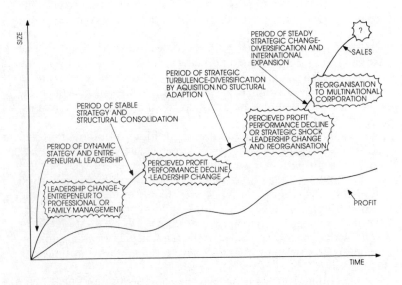

4.2   Channon's model of corporate growth

According to CHANNON a common feature of the revolutionary period is a change of leadership which is precipitated by a decline in profits. At the time of CHANNON's survey all the large construction corporations were led by an entrepreneurial figure who had been involved in the founding of the business. A more recent survey by OGUNLESI (1984) suggests a shift away from entrepreneurial leadership towards professional managers, although the importance of having strong leadership in construction companies is confirmed by O'CALLAGHAN (1986).

Operations
The operations of the building contractor are defined by the nature of the *task* which the organisation performs and the *technology* used. These are important design parameters for the organisation structure.

The *task* performed by a building contractor is part of the total construction process which is necessary to complete a building project. This total process has been described in such documents as the *RIBA Plan of Work* (1973). The building contractor's contribution to this process has traditionally, under competitive tendering methods, been confined to production activities on building sites, although the advent of less orthodox procurement approaches, such as design and build and management contracting, will inevitably enlarge that role.

The traditional role of the building contractor was succinctly described by GRUMMIT (1968) as:

- **getting the work** – this involves estimating and marketing/public relations/sponsorship type activities
- **doing the work** – entailing site management, purchasing materials, plant management, safety, planning, work study, etc, described in chapters 3, 4 and 6.
- **getting paid for the work** – the role of the surveyor and accountant are crucial in ensuring the good cash management described in chapter 7.

Most building organisation's activities are divided broadly along these lines. A company undertaking design and build will need to add a design function and the management contractor will perform a more managerial and less technical role in the process.

The importance of *technology* as a determinant of organisation structure has been stressed by TRIST *et al.* (1963), WOODWARD (1965) and PERROW (1970).

The *socio-technical* approach pioneered by TRIST and others at the Tavistock Institute emphasises the interactive nature of people's motivation and technology. The design of work groups should match the technology employed if productivity is to be maintained. In the construction industry the balancing of gangs with construction operations is a feature of good management.

WOODWARD's research classified a range of firms into *unit* (or small batch), *mass* (or large batch), or *process* (fully automated). She found that the length of the line of command, the span of control of the chief executive, the percentage of turnover devoted to wages and salaries, the ratio or managers to others, of graduates to non-graduates and indirect to direct labour, all increased as the level of technology went from unit to mass or process.

This analysis would suggest that building contracting firms would use unit level technology verging on mass level technology for large housing development schemes, particularly where a high degree of pre-fabrication is present. Therefore, the organisation structure that might be anticipated for a building contractor would exhibit short lines of command, ie few levels of management, narrow span of control of the chief executive, relatively small numbers of managers, graduates and indirect labour. This appears to be so for small and medium sized builders.

A parallel classification of technology is described by LANSLEY (1974) who defines three stages of technological development – *pre-mechanisation*, *mechanisation* and *post-mechanisation*, which are similar to WOODWARD's three categories. He suggests that the majority of tasks on a building site would fall into the pre-mechanisation category with industrialised building perhaps just qualifying as mechanised. He relates technology to the appropriate degree of *control*, where control is defined as 'the extent to which the activities of managers and supervisors are laid down by senior management and defined by detailed rules and regulations', in other words, the extent to which the organisation is bureaucratic. He argues that highly developed control systems are appropriate when:

(a) the nature of the bulk of the output is such that its properties can be precisely specified and measured

(b) production runs are long: the range of products is few; variations in the characteristics of products in the range are minimal

(c) there is a relatively high degree of mechanisation in the production process.

As building operations do not meet these criteria then a high level of control or bureaucracy is not likely to be appropriate.

Both WOODWARD and LANSLEY demonstrated that firms with appropriate organisation structures will perform better than those with structures which do not match their technology.

PERROW (1970) proposed a continuum for technology from *routine*, where a bureaucratic organisation is appropriate, to *non-routine* where a much more flexible 'organic' organisation is required. Again, it can be argued that building companies tend to use technology best described as non-routine and, therefore, a less rigid structure will be more appropriate.

Technological forces seem to push building firms towards more flexible structures than those adopted by manufacturing companies.

Environment

The nature of the construction environment and its impact on construction firms has already been discussed in chapter 2, particularly its effect on the *culture* of the organisation.

Four characteristics of organisational environment appear to influence the structuring of organisations – stability, complexity, market diversity and hostility (MINTZBERG 1979).

Stability – an organisation's environment can range from *stable* to *dynamic*. Relating this characteristic to the continuum of structures – mechanistic to organic – first defined by BURNS and STALKER (1966), the expected response to a dynamic environment would be an organic organisation structure.

The question then arises to what extent can the construction industry environment be described as dynamic? If the meaning of 'dynamic' is further defined as an uncertain and unpredictable environment then it can be seen that the construction industry exhibits both of these features and, therefore, must be classified as dynamic. The reason an 'organic' organisation is likely to be appropriate is the need for flexibility as argued by LANSLEY (1979), to enable the building firm to respond rapidly to changing circumstances.

Complexity – an organisation's environment may range from *simple* to *complex*. '. . . An environment is complex to the extent that it requires the organisation to have a great deal of sophisticated knowledge about products, customers or whatever'. (MINTZBERG 1979). Clearly construction projects present building firms with a relatively complex environment where it is difficult to comprehend the ramifications of events or decisions even at the project level, let alone at the corporate level.

The response to complexity according to LAWRENCE and LORSCH (1967) and GALBRAITH (1973) must be to *decentralise* decision making to those best able to comprehend the problems. In building firms very significant decisions are made by the site manager as discussed in chapter 3.

Market diversity – the markets of an organisation may range from *integrated* to *diverse*. Figure 3.4 in chapter 3 illustrates the two key aspects of service or market diversity coupled with geographical decentralisation which best describe the options open to the building firm. Another way of defining market diversity in terms of services, clients and geography is shown in figure 3.7.

The research of CHANDLER (1966) and CHANNON (1978), described in chapter 3, has shown that the more diversified the organisation's markets the greater the need for the organisation to split into market-based divisions. NEWCOMBE has also demonstrated in FELLOWS *et al.* (1983) that geographical decentralisation by construction firms usually entails the establishing of regional offices to create a local presence. Many of the larger construction corporations have a multi-divisional structure on which are super-imposed regional centres of operation. These divisions and regions are often profit centres, which pushes profit responsibility further down the organisation.

A constraint on complete divisionalisation is a *critical function* which is often common to all markets (CHANNON 1978). Thus, a multi-divisional construction company may still retain central head office responsibility for functions such as personnel, legal and land purchase.

Hostility – an organisation's environment can range from *favourable* and *hostile*. Hostile environments are characterised by the unpredictability of demand, fierce competition and the scarcity of resources; all these factors are clearly evident in the construction industry.

The main requirement in a hostile environment is speed of response which is again a feature of organic organisations. A further response to hostility may be the temporary centralisation of decision making within the organisation. This allows firms to achieve the necessary speed of response because one individual or a small group will make decisions more quickly than is possible in a democratic structure. Democracy and participation may improve morale, but can be a very slow process.

The combination of complexity, forcing the organisation to decentralise, and hostility, which requires centralisation, can set up irreconcilable forces within an organisation. Centralisation may be sustained for a short period, but the pressures of a complex environment may eventually overwhelm the business. The recent recession in the construction industry created conditions of extreme hostility which many building firms did not survive.

Stakeholders
In a sense, everyone associated with the business is a *stakeholder*. The key *external stakeholders* have been discussed in chapter 3 as

part of the firm's competitive environment – suppliers, clients, competitors and new entrants to the firm's markets. To these may be added bankers, financiers, shareholders, central and local government, pressure groups, trades unions, etc.

Whilst these external stakeholders may exert strong influences on the organisation system, the primary sources of power to shape the organisation are the *internal stakeholders* – the directors, managers and employees of the business. Of these, some will exercise more control over the organisation than others; it is, therefore, important to identify the *key* internal stakeholders who can influence the structure of the business by asking:

- who are they?
- what do they want?
- what can they do?
- what can the organisation do?

Who are they?

In terms of shaping the organisation an important aspect is whether the business is *dependent* or *independent* of external control. If a firm is *dependent* on a parent company for finance and direction then research has shown that the organisation will be more formalised and centralised in its structure (PUGH 1969). In other words, dependence tends to encourage bureaucracy and reduce autonomy in decision making. Independent ownership allows organisations more autonomy and the ability, although not necessarily the desire, to decentralise decisions down the hierarchy. The majority of building companies in the UK are still independently owned, but there is a trend towards the formation of groups of companies through the strategy of acquisition.

CYERT and MARCH (1963) assert that:

Organisations do not have objectives; only people have objectives.

This statement stresses the *role* of powerful individuals and groups within the organisation whose *relationship* is described as that of a 'shifting, multi-goal coalition'. 'Shifting' because the importance of members and groups will rise and wane; 'Multi-goal' recognises that members will often hold conflicting objectives; 'coalition' because this most accurately describes the way in which members retain conflicting objectives and principles, but manage to work together.

What do they want?

People have expectations that the organisation will meet some of their needs. The nature of individual and group needs and the motivational devices for meeting them are the subject of chapter 6.

The needs for stability, security, affiliation, status and self-development (MASLOW 1954) have all-pervading implications for the design of the organisation system. The extent of centralisation, standardisation, formalisation, job definition, grouping of people and culture are all influenced by the expectations of the internal stakeholders.

What can they do?

For people to translate their needs into organisational imperatives there are three pre-requisites described by LAWLESS (1979):

- *resources* – they must control resources, whether these are physical, financial or personal
- *dependency* – the value of a resource is not determined solely by its possession, but by the extent to which other people are dependent upon using that resource
- *alternatives* – the extent of dependence will obviously be influenced by the availability of alternatives to the user of the resources.

An example of this power of stakeholders in building organisations is strike action by operatives who withdraw a resource – their skills – which can force changes in the organisation if there is a high dependence on their skills; management may choose to bring in alternative labour, eg sub-constractors. As already mentioned, financial dependence on a parent organisation may force structural changes on an organisation.

What can the organisation do?

Organisations must be designed to take account of the needs, aspirations and power of key people; any action may be mitigated by the other forces – age and size, environment and technology.

The way in which the organisation handles these forces is the subject of the next section.

4.4   The conversion process

As shown in figure 4.1, the conversion process of the organisation system comprises three sub-systems:

- a structural process
- a social process
- a power process.

Whilst for purposes of analysis these three processes will be treated separately, it is important to realise that in reality they are interdependent. A change in the structure will have social and power ramifications and vice versa.

The structural process can be a deliberate design process (but often isn't); the social and power processes evolve.

The structural process
As indicated by the definition of the Primary Task of the organisation system, there are two countervailing forces present in all organisations – *differentiation* and *integration*.

First, the need to divide up the work of the organisation between its members is called *differentiation*. Examples are *horizontal decentralisation* of responsibility, eg the creation of functional departments or market based divisions, and *vertical differentiation*, eg the establishing of levels of management to form a hierarchy.

Second, the force of differentiation generates the need for co-ordination of the differentiated activities; this force is called *integration*. Examples are the appointment of heads of department whose role is to co-ordinate the actions of their subordinates as well as liaison with other parts of the organisation.

Differentiation is necessary in order that the building company can handle the environmental, operational, technological and stakeholder needs described under inputs. Size and environmental complexity for example require horizontal decentralisation to reduce the total task of the business to comprehensible activities.

LAWRENCE and LORSCH (1967) studied organisations and their environments and concluded that environmental uncertainty caused organisations to differentiate their structures with the concomitant need for greater integration.

To design an effective organisation, these two forces must be matched, taking into account the inputs.

Differentiation
Decisions about differentiation need to answer the following questions:

- who does what?
- who reports to whom?
- how much centralisation?
- how shall activities be grouped?

Who does what?
Given the total task that an organisation has to do, the problem is to allocate activities to people whilst ensuring that there are no gaps or overlaps in responsibilities.

This poses two problems:

- how much *specialisation*?
- how much *definition*?

In a small, one-man building business, there is no job specialisation – everything is done by a single individual. As organisations grow and change the trend is toward greater job specialisation. A building company will employ experts in estimating, surveying, accounting, plant, materials, safety, etc, because the environmental, technological and operational complexities force the firm to specialise. A large number of these experts provide advice to line management, for example, an estimator pricing variations or a plant manager advising a site manager on the choice of excavator. Even within line management job specialisation can occur, with site activities specialised by geographic zone or stage of work, eg finishing foreman. At the operative level in the construction industry there has been considerable job specialisation, particularly with the recent increase in sub-contracting. Specialisation can be considered at the corporate, business or project levels and in each case has considerable implications for structure.

The second problem is *job definition*. Will jobs be closely or loosely prescribed? The advantages of a precise job description are:

- responsibilities and authority are clear
- a basis exists for assessing performance
- gaps and overlaps should be avoided if job descriptions are carefully co-ordinated.

There are disadvantages, in that:

- it may not be appropriate to closely specify jobs in small organisations where job flexibility is crucial. The majority of building firms are small
- the wording of the job description can be used as a weapon in 'work to rule' disputes
- flexible use of people is destroyed
- job description may become out of date
- closely prescribed jobs limit individual freedom and initiative.

Many companies find the solution to this problem in Management by Objectives which is explained in chapter 7.

Job specialisation and job definition decisions primarily affect the *horizontal differentiation* of the organisation.

Who reports to whom?

Two problems have to be solved:

- the span of control
- the unity of command.

The classical theorists were particularly concerned about the number of subordinates that a manager had to control, even going as far as to suggest a maximum of five–seven as preferable. However, JOAN WOODWARD (1965) in her study of industrial managers found spans of control of fifty, so that it is clear there is no ideal number of subordinates that a manager can control; it depends on:

- the ability of the manager
- the abilities of the subordinates
- the nature of the work – whether routine or 'one-off'
- the geographical dispersion of subordinates
- the extent to which the work of subordinates is inter-dependent.

Although the last three factors would suggest that narrow spans of control should prevail in construction firms, in practice the ability and need for autonomy of the managers is matched by a similar degree of independence in the largely craft-based work force (LANSLEY 1974). This leads to wide spans of control in building firms and on construction sites.

The importance of span of control is that it directly effects the number of levels of management in the hierarchy. The narrower the span of control the taller the organisational pyramid and vice versa. Building organisations generally favour wider spans of control and flatter structures.

The reciprocal of the problem of the span of control is the number of bosses each subordinate should have. Again, the classical writers urged the tenet that no subordinate should have more than one superior to whom he/she reported. The principle of *unity of command* states that a clear chain of command should exist from the top to the bottom of the organisation and that, in theory, requests upwards from subordinates for decisions and directives from superiors should go up and down the line of command. If this process is strictly followed then the speed of response will be slowed as people at the top of the hierarchy become over-loaded with decision making.

The need for lateral relationships between staff to overcome this problem is recognised by allowing informal liaison to occur outside the formal line of command or by the formal creation of lateral relationships as discussed under integration later in the chapter.

Decisions about span of control and unity of command effect the *vertical differentiation* of the structure.

How much centralisation?
The problem of how much centralisation must be resolved in three areas:

- decision making
- common services
- line and staff relationships.

The first two areas are forms of vertical centralisation; the last area involves horizontal centralisation.

Decision making can be centralised to a single person or a few key individuals or widely dispersed throughout the organisation. The centralisation of decision making should ensure that decisions are consistent and co-ordinated and avoid the problems of conflicting decisions. Equally, the accountability for decisions is clear, a device often used by parent organisations in making the chief executive of the subsidiary company solely accountable for the performance of the company.

Problems which may arise with centralised decision making are that it often produces late or inappropriate decisions. This is a particular problem in the construction industry with geographically dispersed sites coupled with unpredictable events which demand unique decisions. This creates pressure to decentralise decision making to those best able to make the decisions – the site managers, surveyors, site engineers and other functional personnel.

The advantages are that decisions will be made more quickly, they will be relevant to the situation and, because of the autonomy staff feel that they have, should provide greater motivation. In addition, delegating decision making can be used to train subordinates for higher positions in the company.

Common services are another form of centralisation. For example, a site will need a range of services such as surveying, plant, materials supply, programming, accounting, engineering, etc. The services that each site needs could be located on site, but this may not be economical on any but the largest projects. It is, therefore, likely that most building organisations will centralise certain key services in order to develop greater expertise, achieve uniform standards across the organisation, take advantage of economies of scale, eg bulk purchasing, and provide better career opportunities for staff within a specialist discipline. As with all centralisation, there may be a price to pay in slowness of response, breakdowns in communication between head office and site and the fact that the service offered may not meet the need. A prime source of conflict in building organisations is in the poor relationship between sites and the head office service departments.

Line and staff positions in an organisation create a form of horizontal decentralisation. The distinction between 'line' personnel and 'staff' personnel is commonly used in organisations to distinguish between the line people without whom the product or service would not reach the client, and the staff members whose contribution is indirect in the form of advice and assistance to line managers. MINTZBERG's (1979) model of the component parts of an

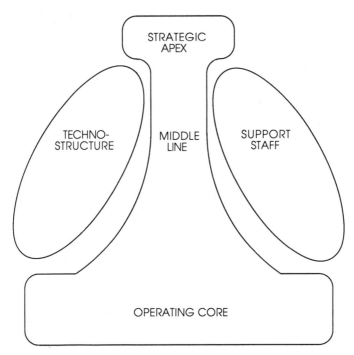

Component parts of organisation

organisation (figure 4.3) is helpful in distinguishing between the line managers at three levels – strategic apex, middle line, operating core – and two groups of staff personnel – the *technostructure* and the *support staff*.

Typical line management positions in a building company would be managing director (*strategic apex*), contracts manager (*middle line*), site managers (*operating core*). Staff departments would include personnel, programming, safety (*technostructure*) and legal, accounting and research (*support staff*).

The dilemma created by line and staff divisions within an organisation is the extent to which the staff members have the authority to enforce their advice on line managers. For example, should the company safety officer be able to close a site if unsafe working practices persist? Any decentralisation of authority from line managers to staff members is likely to be strongly resisted. Equally, if the advice of staff departments is constantly ignored by line managers this will lead to the demotivation of staff personnel. If conflict is to be avoided some sort of balance must be achieved.

How shall activities be grouped?
Very few activities in organisations are carried out by individuals;

most tasks require a group of people to share their skills so that the principal building block of the organisational superstructure is the unit group. The appropriate grouping of activities is, therefore, essential if the organisation is to operate effectively; but on what basis shall activities be grouped? MINTZBERG (1979) identifies four basic criteria that organisations use to select the bases for grouping:

- workflow interdependencies
- process interdependencies
- scale interdependencies
- social interdependencies.

Workflow interdependencies – If people's work requires them to interact with each other on a frequent basis then it makes sense to group them together regardless of their basic discipline. For example, a building project may require that site management and the surveyors co-ordinate their activities closely on competitively priced contracts, or site management and materials management. It may be sensible in these cases to group the different disciplines under the direction of the contracts manager to ensure effective integration. The workflow, as in these cases, is often the project construction process.

Process interdependencies – refer to the necessity for specialists to co-ordinate their activities and to pool their knowledge and experience. An example would be the need for surveyors on different projects to operate the same budgetary control systems. Such considerations may over-ride workflow dependencies.

Scale interdependencies – occur as a result of centralisation decisions discussed earlier. To achieve economies of scale there may be a minimum viable size of group. The allocation of a plant maintenance engineer to a single site may be wasteful in terms of low utilisation and duplication of tools and equipment. The purchase of sophisticated testing equipment may only be justified by the continuous use afforded by making it a centralised facility.

Social interdependencies arise paradoxically in the extreme conditions of danger and boredom. The TRIST and BAMFORTH (1963) study in the coal mines clearly showed the importance of social support and interaction in a dangerous environment. Construction sites, as official statistics regularly reveal, are equally hazardous places in which to work; hence the widespread use of gangs or teams of operatives and staff. Boring and repetitive work will drive people to greater social interaction to relieve the boredom. Although construction work is generally not repetitive, there are inevitably repetitive tasks to be done, in accounting for instance. In these situations it may be important to group people in order to encourage a degree of social interaction.

Most organisation structures are a compromise between the 'objective' requirements of workflow, process and scale and the 'subjective' pressures of social and personal needs.

These criteria will lead companies to select particular bases for grouping.

Bases for grouping

MINTZBERG (1979) points to six bases for grouping which appear in the management literature, to which may be added a seventh of particular significance to construction firms.

1 Grouping by knowledge and skill

This is simply the grouping by discipline, eg all the estimators together, or by level of skill, eg craftsmen and labourers or strategists and operational managers.

2 Grouping by work process and function

The commonest example of this is the functional departments in business organisations – marketing, construction, finance, etc.

3 Grouping by time

STEWART (1970) discusses this basis of grouping which occurs when shift-work is in operation. This may arise on some construction projects where speed of completion is paramount.

4 Grouping by output

These are usually product or market based groups. A construction firm may have a unit producing concrete blocks (product) or a civil engineering division (market).

5 Grouping by client

It is common for construction companies to allocate certain groups to look after particular clients. If a client is continuously employing the firm then a permanent group may be established which is dedicated to that client.

6 Grouping by location

Large construction companies often expand geographically as discussed in chapter 3 by creating regional offices in the UK and/or overseas.

7 Grouping by project

A special case of grouping by location in the construction industry is the appointment of people to project teams.

Most building firms would use a combination of these methods of grouping; for instance, a civil engineering project in the Scottish region for a continuing client where shift-working was present would encompass most of the categories.

The method of grouping will probably vary with the *level* of the company. At the *corporate* level in large organisations grouping will be by output, eg market division and/or by location, eg regional offices, with head offices services grouped by knowledge and skill, eg accountants.

At the *business* level the most common grouping is by function, eg estimating, plant, purchasing, etc.

A further sub-division within each Strategic Business Unit will be by *project*. A typical organisation chart for a large construction corporation is shown in figure 4.4.

Integration
Following or in parallel with decisions about how to divide up the work of the organisation must come decisions about how to ensure co-ordination or integration of the activities. The more complex the organisation's activities the more difficult it will be to co-ordinate them.

Three key factors contribute to the complexity of the organisation's activities:

- differentiation
- inter-dependence of unit groups
- uncertainty.

The sources and bases of *differentiation* have been discussed in the last section and there is much evidence (in addition to common sense) to support the notion that the greater the differentiation the greater the need for integration.

THOMPSON (1967) has shown that three forms of inter-dependence exist between people within organisations as illustrated in figure 4.5.

Pooled inter-dependence is such as exists between building sites and between sites and head office. The sites operate independently and contact with head office departments may be very routine. The need for integration between the sites and between sites and head office will be low.

Sequential inter-dependence occurs where one activity is dependent upon another being completed first. The estimator cannot complete the pricing of the bills of quantitites until he has the materials costs from the purchasing department. More integration is required than for pooled inter-dependence.

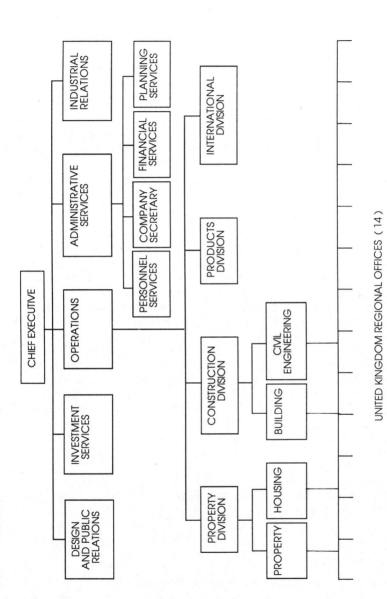

UNITED KINGDOM REGIONAL OFFICES (14)

4.4   *Organisation chart for a large construction corporation*

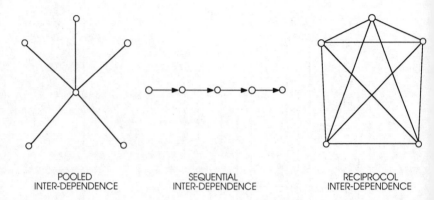

POOLED
INTER-DEPENDENCE

SEQUENTIAL
INTER-DEPENDENCE

RECIPROCOL
INTER-DEPENDENCE

4.5   Types of organisation interdependence

Reciprocal inter-dependence implies continuous interaction between people or groups within an organisation. A design and build contractor's presentation of the company's scheme to a client panel will require considerable co-ordination.

Where services are centralised there will exist reciprocal inter-dependence between service departments and building sites.

Uncertainty is a third important factor in complexity. The more uncertainty there is about clients' actions, staff reactions, sub-contractors, material suppliers, political and economic changes, etc, the more complex the activities of the organisation will seem.

Facing a continuous flow of unpredictable events will increase the need for explicit co-ordination of activities.

As there are bases for differentiation so there are bases for integration.

Bases for integration

Three usual bases for integration described by KAST and ROSENZWEIG (1985) are:

- directive
- voluntary
- facilitated.

Directive integration comes from two sources.

First, the *chain of command* within the hierarchy gives the authority to superiors to direct the activities of their subordinates to ensure co-ordination. A head of department within a building firm typically fulfils this role. In a smaller building firm organised on functional lines the Managing Director directs the co-ordination of the heads of department. As we have seen already, this may lead to over-loading the superior with decision making and consequent inefficiency.

Second, directive integration can be achieved by using *administrative routines or standardisation.*

Administrative routines establish decision rules for recurring events so that co-ordination is effected by people following the known routine procedures. Accounting procedures are common in building firms. This can dramatically reduce the workload of superiors.

Standardisation involves designing work processes, inputs and outputs to achieve co-ordination automatically.

MINTZBERG (1979) is helpful in defining these three forms of standardisation:

Standardisation of work processes
'Work processes are standardised when the contents of the work are specified or programmed.'

Some site operations eg bricklaying and carpentry, are co-ordinated in this way as are administrative activities such as checking invoices.

Standardisation of outputs
'Outputs are standardised when the results of the work, for example the dimensions of the product or the performance, are specified.'

Performance standards are well known in the construction industry and mean that integration is achieved because interfaces between tasks are predetermined. Standardised drawings and schedules from consultants to contractor are an example.

Standardisation of skills
'Skills (and knowledge) are standardised when the kind of training required to perform the work is specified.'

The professional institutions in the construction industry such as the CIOB, the RIBA and the RICS, see this form of standardisation as one of their main roles. Co-ordination automatically results from the parties knowing, as a result of training, precisely what their role entails and how it dovetails into the work of others.

Voluntary integration (what MINTZBERG calls *mutual adjustment*) occurs when people co-ordinate their work with others by the simple process of informed communication. In small organisations there are many face-to-face encounters between people when co-ordination issues are resolved. This is one way of over-coming the slowness of the proper operation of the chain of command. A site

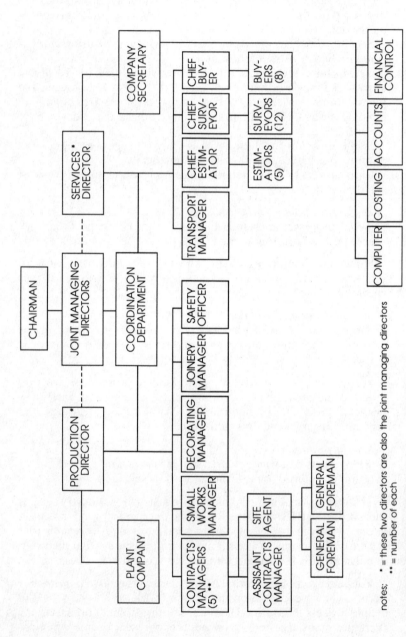

notes: * = these two directors are also the joint managing directors
          ** = number of each

4.6 *Organisation chart for a medium sized building contractor*

manager may go to see an estimator to discuss the price for an item of work without going through his contracts manager.

Facilitated integration is obtained by the deliberate creation of liaison devices within the organisation structure. GALBRAITH (1973) proposed a continuum of liaison devices, four of which are considered below.

Standing committees are permanent groups super-imposed on the existing structure. An example is shown in figure 4.6 of a co-ordination committee created within a building contracting firm to co-ordinate the activities of those involved in a project from estimate to completion. People are seconded to this committee for specific projects.

Task forces, unlike standing committees, are set up for a specific project or undertaking. For example, a building firm preparing to take over another firm may establish a task force to handle the merger. When the merger is complete the team will be disbanded.

'Linking pins' is a concept suggested by LIKERT (1967) and illustrated in figure 4.7. Key individuals are designated liaison positions within the structure both horizontally between groups and vertically between levels.

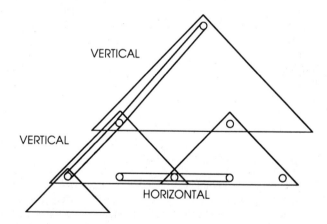

4.7 Linking pin patterns

Matrix structures are by far the most sophisticated of the liaison devices discussed so far. It involves a fundamental redesign of the organisation structure by superimposing task forces or project teams onto a functional structure, as shown in figure 4.8.

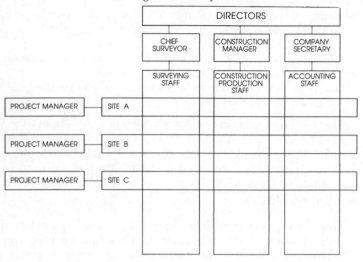

4.8   Matrix organisation structure

The design creates two chains of command, with individuals being temporarily seconded from functional departments to join multi-disciplinary teams under the direction of a project manager. The dual authority of the project manager and the functional manager contravenes the tenet of unity of command and may cause stress to the subordinate. There are other benefits and problems associated with this form of organisation which are comprehensively covered in KNIGHT (1976).

In a project-based industry like construction, matrix organisations are common, but should not be used where simpler liaison devices will provide the necessary integration.

The output of the structural process will be a structural configuration. Five such configurations will be considered under the outputs section of this chapter.

The social process

As we have seen the structural process creates formal permanent and temporary groups. This may be by design or by evolution.

The *social process* also produces groups of people, but such groups are rarely designed, rather they evolve in response to human needs. Such social groups make up the *informal organisation*.

SCHEIN (1980) provides a good review of the way in which the social process operates. He points out that:

'. . . members of organisations are formally called upon to provide only certain activities in order to fulfil their organisational role. But, because the whole person actually reports for work or joins the organisation, and because people have needs beyond the minimum ones of doing their job, they will seek fulfilment of some of those needs through developing a variety of relationships with other members of the organisation.'

MASLOW's (1954) higher level needs – security, esteem, self-actualisation – as well as the need for affiliation and for power may be met through the social structure.

Certain factors will determine the way in which the social process operates which SCHEIN classifies as *environmental* factors, *membership* factors and *dynamic* factors.

Environmental factors refer firstly to the nature of the work itself, ie whether it encourages or discourages interaction between people, the location of people, the time schedules that they work and so on. The appointment of people to a contractor's team on a building site will almost certainly lead to the formation of an informal group.

The second environmental influence is the attitude of management, who may encourage or actively discourage the social process, depending on their views about the value of a social structure.

Membership factors depend on the composition of the group. The attitudes, values and beliefs of individuals as well as their abilities will strongly influence the social process.

Dynamic factors are those factors associated with the formation and growth of informal groups – leadership styles, organisation structure, communications, the time that people have for interaction.

The relationship between the structural process and the social process has been traced by HOMANS (1950). He developed a model of social systems which contained three elements. *Activities* are the tasks that people perform. *Interactions* are the behaviours that occur between people in performing these tasks.

Sentiments are the attitudes that develop between individuals and within groups. HOMANS argues that although these concepts are separate, they are closely inter-related as shown in figure 4.9.

A change in one of these three elements will produce a change in the other two. The way in which the model operates in practice is that people are allocated jobs (*activities*) by the structural process that requires them to work together (*interactions*). These jobs must be sufficiently satisfying (*sentiments*) for people to continue doing them. As people interact through their jobs so they will develop sentiments towards each other. The more people interact the more

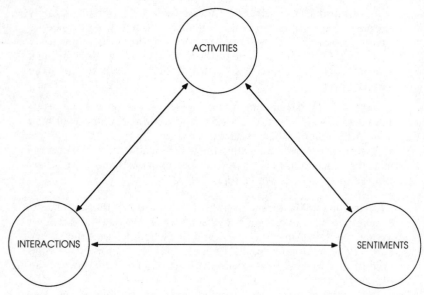

4.9   A model of the social process

positive will become the sentiments between them and this will lead them to interact even more. Increasing interaction will cause them to become more alike in their activities and sentiments so that group norms develop. These norms will reinforce the group's power over its members and the group's power over others. This anatomy of the interaction of the structural and social systems is helpful in understanding the social structure. The nature of the social structure will be discussed under outputs. Some of the aspects of the social process are treated more fully in chapter 6.

The power process
The power process has been obliquely referred to in chapter 3 and also in this chapter. Just as the formal structure encourages the formation of a social structure, so it also creates a *power structure* through a *power process*.

The centralisation or decentralisation of decision making, discussed under structure earlier in the chapter, is the key to understanding power within organisations. In organisational terms power can be defined as the *power to influence decisions*. We have already seen that power over decisions can be centralised to a single point in the organisation or can be decentralised or dispersed to many individuals. Three forms of decentralisation are evident in construction companies:

- *vertical* decentralisation refers to the dispersal of power down the chain of command
- *horizontal* decentralisation refers to the extent to which staff personnel, as opposed to line managers, control the decision-making process
- *spatial or geographical* decentralisation is defined as the extent to which power to make decision is given to geographically dispersed sites.

The distribution of power within the organisation can thus occur in a number of ways:

- vertical decentralisation with horizontal centralisation would result in all the power residing with the site managers
- horizontal decentralisation with vertical centralisation would pass the power to senior staff people
- centralisation of both would mean that top management retain the power
- decentralisation of both would distribute power widely throughout the business.

The way in which power is distributed between the members of the organisation will create a unique power structure. Two ostensibly similar organigrams can carry completely different power structures.

It follows from what has already been said that the power process is closely linked to the decision making process. PATERSON (1969) illustrates this link as shown in figure 4.10.

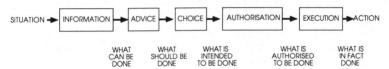

| SITUATION → | INFORMATION | → | ADVICE | → | CHOICE | → | AUTHORISATION | → | EXECUTION | →ACTION |

| | WHAT CAN BE DONE | WHAT SHOULD BE DONE | WHAT IS INTENDED TO BE DONE | WHAT IS AUTHORISED TO BE DONE | WHAT IS IN FACT DONE |

4.10   A continuum of control over the decision process

The steps involved are:

- collecting *information* about what is feasible or *can* be done
- offering *advice* on what *should* be done
- making a *choice* of the best or at least the most acceptable, solution
- seeking *authorisation* for the decision
- the *execution* of a particular decision.

Another way of viewing the centralisation/decentralisation issue is to realise that the more control an individual or group exercises over these steps the more centralised is the power to that individual or group. As others become involved in the steps so the power process devolves to those people. Maximum power rests with the individual when he collects his own information, analyses it himself, makes the choice, seeks no authorisation and executes it himself.

The power process is dispersed when others can filter information, offer selected advice, control authorisation of courses of action and decide how, when and if the decision is to be executed.

It can be seen that an organisation where power to *make* decisions is centralised can actually have a decentralised power structure if others control and manipulate parts of the decision process.

The output of this power process will be a power structure to be discussed under outputs.

4.5 Outputs

There are three outputs from the three conversion processes of the organisation system as shown in figure 4.1:

–   the authority structure
–   the social structure
–   the power structure.

The authority structure
The authority structure is the formal arrangement of roles and relationships which arise from decisions about differentiation and integration. It is often presented in the form of an organisation chart or organigram as in figures 4.4 and 4.6.

A more general classification of structural configurations has been developed by MINTZBERG (1979) based on a large-scale synthesis of the research and thinking about organisations. MINTZBERG identified five types of authority structure and showed that the appropriate structure for an organisation is influenced by the contingency factors of age and size, technology, environment and stakeholders needs; these have been termed 'inputs' in this chapter. The five structural configurations and the influence of the contingency factors are illustrated in figure 4.11.

Structural configurations
Located at the points of the pentagon are five pure types of authority structure which are variations of the MINTZBERG model shown in figure 4.3. These are defined by IIRWIG (1984):

The simple structure – characterised by centralised authority exerting direct supervision over a set of relatively undifferentiated activities.

Typically, a small or newly formed building firm would have these characteristics.

The *professional bureaucracy* – characterised by considerable delegation of authority, along professional and trade lines and relatively little direct supervision.

Building firms organised as co-operatives or architectural practices will probably be of this type.

The *machine bureaucracy* – identifiable because of the division of work along strictly functional lines and the reliance placed on standardisation of procedures for the co-ordination and control of activities.

The medium sized building contractor shown in figure 4.6 is typical of this configuration although it is not a pure type.

The *divisional structure* – characterised by the fragmentation of the organisation into market-related segments which are relatively independent of each other and of central headquarters.

The majority of large construction corporations are organised in this way. Figure 4.4 shows a large contractor with a divisional structure.

The *adhocracy* – characterised by the delegation of authority along matrix lines, the existence of project groups and the informality of co-ordination within these groups.

A range of construction companies are organised as adhocracies. A matrix structure is illustrated in figure 4.8.

Contingency factors
The effects of the contingency factors on structural configurations which have been discussed under 'inputs', are shown as exerting a number of 'pulls' in figure 4.11.
IIRWIG (1984) defines the effects as follows:

Age and size – increases in organisational size tends to pull the structure of the organisation downward on the pentagon, around its left side. Age, on the other hand, tends to pull organisations to the upper middle – level of the pentagon which is characterised by the bureaucratic mode.

Technology – sophistication and automation of the technical system both tend to pull the organisational configuration to the right of the pentagon and downwards, subject to the constraint that the technical system does not strongly control or regulate the work of members of the organisation. In such situations, there is a pull to the left, towards the bureaucratic level of the pentagon.

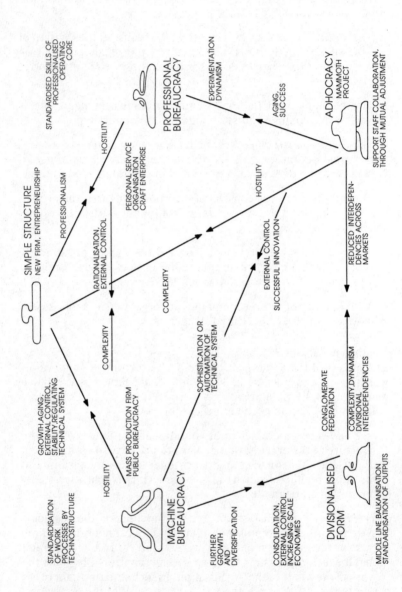

4.11 *Mintzberg's pentagon*

Environment – a *dynamic* environment, in which changes occur unexpectedly with little or no advance warning and make the work unpredictable, tends to pull the organisational configuration to the bottom right corner of the pentagon. Environmental *hostility*, as evidenced by intense competition or scarce resources, requires fast responses and tends to pull an organisation's structure in the opposite direction, towards the type appearing at the top of the pentagon, the simple structure. *Complex* organisational environments, requiring that enterprises have a great deal of sophisticated knowledge to perform the work, tend to pull the structure to the right of the pentagon, towards a more horizontally decentralised system. *Diversity* of the environment, on the other hand, exerts a pull towards the lower left of the pentagon, towards the divisionalised form of organisation which can better cope with a variety of different contexts.

Stakeholders' needs – External control of an organisation, resulting from the need to ensure the security of resources provided it, tends to pull the configuration to the left side, upper-middle, bureaucratic level of the pentagon. The power needs of the organisation's members tend to draw the organisation to that configuration which gives the members what they are looking for; for instance, professional independence in the case of highly trained technical personnel, and tight control in the case of top managers at the strategic apex.

IRWIG (1984) used the MINTZBERG pentagon to study six construction contractors operating in Cleveland, USA. The research attempted to answer two key questions:

1 How do the organisational configurations of construction firms relate to those of other enterprises?
2 Do construction firms behave in a similar fashion to those situational factors which have been shown to influence organisation structures and procedures?

Of the six construction firms in the sample, the two smallest companies with long histories had a simple structure, two larger companies were located between the simple structure and the adhocracy, the largest company's configuration closely resembled an Adhocracy, and the last firm was in fact a group of smaller companies formed through mergers and acquisitions which was run through a divisionalised structure. The absence of the bureaucractic forms confirms STITCHCOMBE's (1959) assertion that construction companies do not employ bureaucractic co-ordinating mechanisms. With this exception the conclusion is that construction firms exhibit a relatively wide range of organisational configurations. The 'pulls' of the contingency factors in the construction contractors were consistent with those indicated in the pentagon for firms in general.

This small study seems to confirm that certain authority structures are used by construction firms in response to the contingency factors or inputs described earlier in the chapter.

The social structure

By definition the *informal* social structure is unlikely to appear on the organisation chart, but is just as surely present. Three types of informal group or clique have been found in organisations (SCHEIN 1980).

The most prevalent are *horizontal cliques* which comprise managers and other members who are more or less at the same hierarchical level in the business and who work in the same geographical location. In a building organisation the Chief Estimator, Chief Surveyor, Construction Manager, Plant Manager and Company Secretary might form a horizontal clique.

A second type of informal group is the *vertical clique* composed of members from different levels within a particular department. It is usual for only certain members of a department to belong to the clique, often based on the earlier acquaintance of the people involved. In construction companies it is common for directors to have been formerly tradesmen and retain links with former fellow operatives who are still 'on the tools'. This can create friction if an operative can overturn a decision by his site manager by virtue of access to a director of the firm.

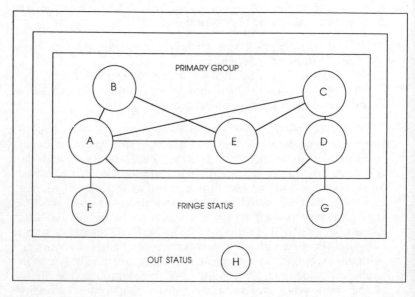

4.12   A sociogram

The third type of informal group, called a *random or mixed clique*, is comprised of members from different levels, from different departments and from different locations. This type of informal relationship is often used to short-circuit formal communication channels as, for example, when the Chief Executive seeks information about a performance standard directly from a site manager that he knows well. Such relationships can arise from contacts outside of the organisation as a result of people living in the same area or belonging to the same sports or social club.

A way of charting these types of clique is to observe the pattern of contacts within a group and to use this information to construct a *sociogram*. Alternatively, people can be asked with whom they prefer to work as the basis of a sociogram. A typical sociogram is shown in figure 4.12.

This could be a formal department or site team of eight people, five of whom interact frequently and form the *Primary* group; two members are on the fringe of the group with a single separate contact each; one member is isolated from the group and although this person may formally be a member of the team, in practice he is not in the social structure of the group.

The power structure
The third output of the organisation system is a power structure.

Power within organisations has already been defined as the power to make decisions. The power to make decisions depends upon the *power bases* from which a person operates and the *culture* of the organisation. These together form the *power structure* of the organisation.

Power bases
Seven power bases in organisations have been identified by KAKABADSE (1987):

1 Reward power
Reward power is used by people in a position to influence the rewards which others receive. The power base is the control of material resources, eg financial rewards, or non-material rewards such as status and privilege. The use of incentive schemes at all levels in the construction industry is an indication of the importance of reward power. The power of rewards to motivate people depends, of course, on whether the rewards are perceived by the recipient to be attainable or worthwhile.

2 Coercive power
This power base relies on the ability of the power-holder to mete out punishment. This could range from sarcastic criticism of a

subordinates work to actual dismissal of an individual from the company.

3   Position power
The authority structure creates positions for people and delegates a degree of power to those positions. As already indicated, this power may be closely or loosely prescribed. The person has power because of the position he/she holds, eg a head of department or project manager.

4   Personal power
This power stems from an individual's force of personality, sometimes called *charisma*. This power base operates if others are attracted to a key person and if there is a great deal of inter-personal contact. A person very low in the structural hierarchy may exert considerable personal power over the actions of others.

5   Expert power
A person perceived as possessing specialist knowledge or skills in a particular discipline will be seen to have expert power. A plant engineer, an accountant, or a computer analyst may use this type of power.

6   Information power
This power base is explored in detail in chapter 5, but anyone who collects, filters and disseminates information has the power to withhold or distort the facts. MINTZBERG's (1973) analysis of management work identifies informational roles as one of three key sets of roles which managers fulfill (see chapter 7).

7   Connection power
MINTZBERG again refers to the importance, to a manager, of building a network of contacts both inside and outside the organisation. This network provides a powerful base from which a manager can operate as will be explained in chapter 7.

Organisational cultures
Organisational cultures have already been discussed in chapter 2 in the environmental context; here they are defined as a part of the power structure.

The culture of an organisation is difficult to define, but HANDY (1981) says:

> In organisations, there are deep-set beliefs about the way work should be organised, the way authority should be exercised, people rewarded, people controlled.

Handy goes on to define four cultures (see chapter 2 for a fuller exposition).

The *power culture* is one in which power is wielded by a single individual or by a small group of key people. There are few rules and procedures and little bureaucracy. Personal power together with information and connection power are likely to form major power bases in this culture.

The *role culture* is typified by bureaucracy. The features of bureaucracy – rules, procedures, a clear hierarchy, job descriptions, standardisation, formalisation, etc, give a clear description of the character of this culture. Position power is primarily complimented by reward and coercive power.

The *task culture* is project orientated and is frequently a adhocracy. Multi-disciplinary groups, project teams or task forces are formed for specific purposes and are dismantled and reformed to meet rapidly changing demands. The power base most used is expert power coupled with personal power.

The *people culture* is not common in business for its focus is the individual rather than financial performance. Self-actualisation and individual freedom are the hallmarks of the people culture; power rests with the individual and is shared between members. Expert power is the usual base for action. Some architectural practices and contractor's co-operatives have this type of culture, but it is rare.

Power is the base for action and, therefore, the power structure determines what an organisation does as opposed to what it says it will do.

As argued earlier in the chapter, the ultimate output of the organisation system is operational effectiveness. The sole rationále for an organisation to exist is that it facilitates operational performance; it is a means to an end.

When operational performance declines how do we know which contributory causes stem from the organisation system? This is the reason for motivating relevant feedback.

4.6 Feedback

CHILD (1977) lists a number of what he calls 'consequences of structural dificiencies':

low motivation and morale
late and inappropriate decisions
conflict and lack of co-ordination
rising costs
inadequate response to changing circumstances.

These often occur because of a poorly designed organisation structure; an anti-organisational social structure; a mis-use of power. There may be other reasons for these problems, eg personality clashes, but they seem to be typical of a poorly performing organisation system.

4.7   Summary

Four sets of inputs to the organisation system have been discussed –
age and size, operations, environment and stakeholders. Three
conversion processes are at the core of the system – a structural
process, a social process and a power process.

The three conversion processes take the four inputs and produce
three outputs – an authority structure, a social structure and a
power structure. The ways in which these three structures can be
charted was explained. The ultimate output is operational performance.

Feedback in the form of five symptoms of organisational
deficiencies should help the managers of the organisation system to
recognise and correct problems in the system.

Questions

1   Building companies of all sizes share the necessity to execute
    certain business functions.
        Identify these functions and explain how they may need to
    develop with the growth of a company.
                                CIOB *Building management I* 1986

2   Many theorists have recognised the need to overcome the
    fragmentation caused by decentralisation of industrial organisa-
    tions.
    (a)   Show how the work of any two theorists seeks to overcome
          this fragmentation.
    (b)   Comment upon the applicability of such theoretical
          solutions to a building company.
                                CIOB *Building management II* 1986

3   Organisations may be divided by product, by function or by
    geographical area.
        Evaluate the usefulness of each strategy to a building
    company.
                                CIOB *Building Management II* 1987

4   To get things done, a manager requires power based upon
    rewards, position, personality and expertise.
        Discuss this statement in relation to any selected management
    position within the building industry.
                                CIOB *Building Management II* 1987

5 Information

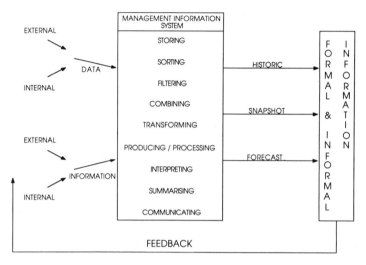

5.1   Information system

5.1   Primary Task

The Primary Task is:

> To collect data and information in order to produce and communicate information to facilitate the efficient operation of the organisation and to ensure compliance with statutory (and similar) requirements.

Information provides 'visibility' for the organisation and its activities.

Introduction
Data are raw facts and figures; *information* is data in a form which is useful to the recipients and should be communicated to them efficiently. Information is used to support decisions; data are used to produce information.

Information is useless unless it is communicated effectively. The total sub-system of management information should strive for production and communication of information not only effectively but also efficiently – a marginal approach (cost or ability) is appropriate.

Figure 5.1 shows the information sub-system. Inputs comprise both data and information. Data generated and collected within the organisation are obtained under the control of the organisation – what the data are, level of detail, frequency of collection, method of sampling, etc. External data are not controlled by the organisation and so it relies on the work of other agencies. The other input is information, both internal and external. The conversion process adapts the inputs to produce the required outputs; a variety of manipulations and interpretations will occur to ensure that the requisite outputs are provided and communicated.

The information which is *output* by the sub-system comprises:

historic information – where the organisation was; how it performed

snapshot information – what was/is the state of the organisation its products, etc, at a particular moment

forecast information – prediction of the organisation's performance in the future.

Outputs are formal and/or informal. Formal outputs often appear as written, official reports, whilst informal outputs frequently are verbal, therefore transient and rather unofficial. The final component of the sub-system is the *feedback loop*. Feedback is vital to inform the operators of the information sub-system how successfully the system is performing in meeting the needs of the managers who use the system's outputs. It is via the information provided by the feedback process that the system can be modified to improve its performance – what is provided, how, when, how rapidly, etc.

Much information is required from companies (and other organisations) under statutes; eg financial accounts, tax returns, articles of association. Such information is *historic* as are most items of information collected for production of government statistics and similar surveys. Other information is *snapshot* – it seeks to answer 'where are we now?' – a balance sheet is of this form. Other information seeks to forecast, eg an estimate.

It is (almost) inevitable that information will contain errors. It is important to appreciate the possibilities, types and sources of the errors and to have some measure (or awareness) of their likely sizes; this is applicable to forecasts especially.

As facilities for data processing increase in speed, capacity and sophistication, there is a tendency for increasing amounts and varieties of information to be demanded and, hence, a proliferation of data production. Although data should be factual, they may be subject to distortions caused by, inter alia, the purposes for which they are collected. There is a distinct danger of management's being swamped by information – too much information can be just as detrimental as too little; managers should determine the information they need for their decision making and obtain that information (in appropriate forms) only.

In the age of computers, these 'machines' often are blamed for errors. Machine-caused errors are rare, it is usually the software (programs) or, most often, human error in inputting which causes the problems; GIGO – garbage in, garbage out – is apposite.

Good communication is essential for an efficient information sub-system. Most people are not very good communicators as they seek to transmit information in ways which suit them, paying little regard to the requirement of the recipient. Communications in the construction industry occur most frequently through speech, writing and drawing; some visual examples are used and electro-magnetic communications media (floppy discs, tapes, etc) are likely to play an increasing role in the future. As there must be compatibility between computer systems and language for trans-mission of data via floppy discs, etc, so there must be similar compatibilities between people to permit them to communicate efficiently.

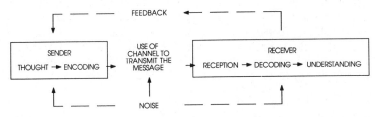

5.2 Communication process model

Figure 5.2 depicts a simple model of communications and figure 5.3 shows the cycle of management information.

The information sub-system must satisfy two basic needs. It must provide information to assist management in problem solving – individual problems often require bespoke inputs to yield the information necessary for their solution; this function must be fulfilled by a reactive capacity in the information sub-system. Management requires information for assistance in taking decisions of a more continuous nature – tactics and strategies. Such policy decisions require both information which has been produced from a proactive stance (it was believed that such information would be helpful/required) and, where possible, forecasts; these functions must be fulfilled by a proactive capacity.

An efficient information sub-system has reactive capacity but also provides sufficient proactive information to facilitate efficient

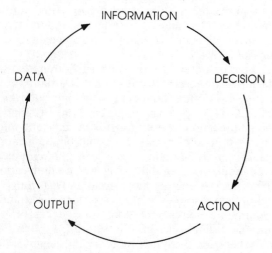

5.3   Cycle for (management) information

managerial decision taking. It is the balance between the two
activities which is important to eliminate idle resources (reactive
capacity waiting for information to be required) and unnecessary
information provision (proactive function collecting all available
data and information and producing a vast array of information,
much of which is not required, and giving management an
enormous task of sorting to obtain the information actually
needed).

5.3   Inputs

The inputs necessary for the information sub-system are determined by the outputs required from the system. DEARDEN (1965)
determined that the three major information classifications for an
organisation are:

    personnel
    logistic
    financial.

He suggested that a further four sub-classifications could be
helpful: *marketing*, *research and development*, *strategic planning*
and *executive compensation*. Whilst all organisations will require
the primary classes of information, this is not so for the secondary
classes – notably, in the UK construction industry research and
development is often omitted (contrast with Japan).

Any information sub-system is only as good as its inputs. Input data and information are historic – records of past activities and performance or predictions of the future which were made some time ago. Updating requirements must not be disregarded, even if no updating is carried out.

Data and information inputs are required in three modes – *occasional*, *continuous* and *periodic*. Occasional inputs occur irregularly, either as part of reactions to problems or situations and, as such, are commissioned internally or are generated externally and are obtained in an ad hoc fashion (reports of studies fall into the latter category, eg NEDO (1983)). Whilst the internal, reactive inputs usually are sought to meet a short term need, the external information frequently concerns strategic, long term issues, applicable to the industry in general.

Periodic inputs occur regularly, at prescribed intervals. External inputs comprise information such as the Budget and data such as Housing and Construction Statistics. Internally generated information and data are provided, for example, in a company's annual report and accounts. Many periodic inputs, especially those generated internally, are geared more to problem avoidance than problem solving and so require forward-looking to the short and medium terms. The externally generated inputs provide information, data and forecasts pertaining to the organisation's environment.

Continuous inputs, in practice, are provided frequently, with only short time intervals between each provision, rather than being truly continuous, eg site labour productivity measures; F/T share indices. Such inputs assist an organisation in coping with environmental and internal variabilities. Occasional and periodic inputs are suited to assist in the reduction of perceived variabilities. Thus, although continuous inputs are instantaneous measures of variables, the information produced by the sub-system from those inputs is medium to long term in nature, often concerned with seeking opportunities for the organisation to exploit (see *Marketing* chapter 12).

In determining the requisite inputs for an information sub-system it is useful to ask, and answer, the following hierarchy of questions:

1 What is the information for?
2 When is the information required?
3 Who is the information for?
4 Why is the information required?
5 Where is the information required?
6 How is the information required?

Questions 1 and 2 are essential. All have implications for the information sub-system itself (inputs-conversions-outputs) and for communications. In particular, the answers affect:

(a)   the levels of accuracy (required), and
(b)   the degree of detail.

It is advisable to use routine and/or automatic data collection when and where possible. Making the data, and their collection, independent of individuals (especially those concerned with the processes in production, etc, which generate the data) helps to avoid bias. Routine collection should result in known levels of accuracy which can be checked against the designed levels of accuracy.

Data

It is becoming increasingly popular, and, probably, essential, to use data for more than one purpose. The suitability of the data for multiple use must be evaluated – it may be preferable to collect data specific to an individual information requirement than to use data which were collected for another purpose and then to transform those data, accepting various biases, inaccuracies and errors, to suit the second use. Thus, whilst the required information outputs determine the data inputs needed, the collection of data should, as far as possible, be an independent activity, carried out to avoid bias and with acceptable accuracy.

Much data arise from sampling, eg production quality controls, and so have inherent potential errors which can be calculated statistically. Generally error reduction requires larger samples and so increases the costs of data collection (marginal analysis will indicate the optimum level of sampling, etc).

As information is a pre-requisite of decision making (see figure 5.3) it must be timely. Determination of the necessary data, their collection and conversion into information are not instantaneous actions. So, as with any system, leads and lags exist; information requirement leads data activities which lead information production.

As data produced externally are not gathered under the control of the organisation, they should be used with care, especially if employed for purposes other than those for which the data were collected. It is likely that methods of collection and accuracies of external data will not be known widely and so, if possible, should be obtained from the agency providing the data. Such data, however, are very helpful in determining trends, eg orders for weekly work, and levels (of activity – output, of costs – Building Cost Index, etc).

For particular purposes it is probable that internal data will be required. Such data have the advantages of being within the control of the organisation and, hence, tailored to the needs of the organisation and of known variability. As such, internal data will form the base of the reactive portion of the sub-system as well as contributing to the proactive portion.

Internal data have the disadvantage of costs being incurred by the organisation and time being necessary for their collection. However, external data are rarely free but are available on subscription, eg Building Cost Information Service or through (special) libraries. Certain external agencies, eg Meteorological Office, will provide data on request for a nominal payment. Others, eg Central Statistical Office, can provide bespoke analyses of the data they have collected. There are, of course, agencies which provide data on a commercial consultancy basis. Bodies, such as departments of universities, are well qualified to provide a whole spectrum of information services from data collection to full research programmes.

Information
Information is data which have been processed into a form which can be used by the recipients. Thus there is some area of ambiguity in deciding when data become information – the nature of the material, its form of presentation, its purpose, what processing has been executed and the recipient's needs and expertise will be relevant. From the view of inputs to an organisation's information sub-system, the differentiation between data and information is not vital; it is usual for both types of input to undergo conversion to yield outputs.

External information comprise reports and similar documents. They may be the results of widely based studies, eg Wood report, of construction operations and contain recommendations for action by the industry, be evaluations of potential/treats, eg 'Japan' study by the University of Reading, or forecasts of immediate, domestic matters, eg Budget reports; long-term weather forecasts. As with external data, external information usually is general, it considers the context in which particular organisations do or may operate. Only when information has been commissioned from an external agency, and thereby 'internalised', will it be really specific to that organisation.

In contrast, internal information is organisation specific, it is a view of, from and by that organisation. Even if the subject is quite general, such as predictive evaluation of the future market for construction work, and so executed objectively, it will contain information specific to the organisation, eg predictions of the organisation's market share.

Internal information, such as the strategic plan, will be employed to produce subsidiary information – prospectuses to accompany new issues of shares; production targets. At the level of individual projects, programming, for example, occurs in a hierarchy from the project's master programme via short-term programmes to schedules of daily production requirements; feedback involves reports on achievements against the plans and should include reasons for any variances.

5.4   The conversion process

Although some inputs may be used directly as information in the organisation, the vast majority require some conversion – data must be converted into information, input information (reports) must be converted into more useful and convenient forms (summaries). Usually, conversion will involve interpretation and, thereby, may introduce distortions whether deliberate (bias) or accidental (error); further, analogous problems may occur in the communications activities.

Conversion is the data and information 'handling' component of the sub-system. Traditionally the functions were carried out by hand but now, and increasingly, computer technology is employed. A result of the change is that computational errors should be reduced, hopefully minimised, but the errors and biases which do remain may be far more difficult to detect and eliminate.

'*To err is human but to really foul things up requires a computer!*' The statement, of course, is a reflection of the capacity of modern computers, especially where one set of data is used to produce a variety of information.

Computers themselves are electronic data/information systems requiring inputs, executing conversions and producing outputs.

Whilst a major objective of using a computer is to save labour and another is to enhance information availability and access, that computer personnel surround themselves with minefields of jargon and mystique tends to detract from the full realisation of the objectives.

Storing

Of the main functions of any information sub-system, only storage of inputs is mechanistic. However, to be efficient, even this apparently simple function must be designed and executed with care and precision and provide facilities for easy verification of the inputs, eg all-in-labour rates to be used for estimating. However executed, the storage files require much space; inputting is a labour intensive operation and so is both time-consuming and where the bulk of the errors occur.

Checking input is a lengthy and costly process but may prevent major errors occurring through provision of mis-information. Also, it is important that the output be scrutinised by someone with knowledge of the inputs and conversions to detect any obvious errors which remain; especially when using automatic data processing the outputs must not be accepted blindly, the scrutineer must be aware at least of the orders of magnitude of the outputs which the inputs should yield, eg inputs of labour rates and materials quotes used to produce Bills of Quantities item rates.

Sorting

Once the inputs have been entered into the sub-system correctly – the process which duplicates as the store of raw inputs – frequently it is necessary to sort the inputs into a form suited to the conversion processes to be executed to yield the required outputs, eg materials quotes. Whether it is preferable to sort the inputs before or after they are stored is a consideration for system design/selection as well as one pertaining to the processing required. Generally it is better to enter store raw inputs and to manipulate them subsequently (to facilitate checking and to pinpoint responsibilities).

Sorting involves selecting those inputs which are required to produce the outputs. If some inputs are not being used they are redundant and so should be discarded, thereby saving on collection and on inputting and storage. Occasional use of inputs which are obtained frequently should be evaluated to decide whether to continue in that mode or subsequently to obtain such inputs as and when required, ie to transfer them from the proactive to the reactive part of the sub-system.

Sorting often involves placing the selected inputs in a second store; normally it is preferable to retain the original input store and to treat the second store as temporary – required until the processing of the selected inputs is complete. Sorting may occur at various stages in the conversion processing, especially where inputs are used for a multiple of outputs, eg site measures of labour productivity can be used for bonus, estimating, site costing, etc.

Filtering

Filtering is a higher level of sorting. Once sorting has occurred – to get inputs into the categories required – filtering may occur to eliminate items within a category. A simple filter is one of minimum or maximum magnitude. Again, a post-filter (temporary) store may be created.

Although filtering can be executed when raw inputs are collected, generally, it is preferable to obtain full sets of inputs and then for the sub-system to perform processes on them internally – thereby control vests in the sub-system alone, eg selecting which supplier to use for facing bricks on a project where several types of bricks are to be used and several suppliers have quoted prices for bricks – need to consider delivery and packaging also.

Combining

Inputs can be combined easily but cannot be disaggregated; this factor is important when deciding what inputs to collect.

It is common for combining to be required when inputs are required for multiple uses eg cost and bonus – productivity – information being used for estimating also. Further, different managerial functions and levels require information in various degrees of detail, higher management requiring less detail. However, it is important to remember that it is not the level of management which determines the detail required but the purpose which the information is required to serve.

Transforming

Transforming usually occurs to data rather than to information. Normally, it is a mathematical process which is employed to express the raw data in a form which is easier to understand. (A common mathematical transformation is to take logarithms of an expotential progression, which yields an arithmetic series – a curve thereby becomes a straight line; another type of transformation is to convert figures into a graph – such as monthly payments on a project.)

Care is needed in dealing with transformed data, particularly in selecting the appropriate transformation(s) and in producing the final information – to ensure that, where necessary, the required reverse transformations are carried out and, in all cases, the meaning of the information is clear; visual aids are useful in this regard.

Producing/Processing

This function comprises analysis of the inputs and production of results. Activities vary from simple additions of numeric inputs, changing formats of inputs, eg producing a graph from a histogram; summarising a report, to complex stochastic forecasting, eg PERT programming and resourcing techniques; Box-Jenkins times series procedures, and other involved techniques.

Obviously the use of computers facilitates much quicker processing at reasonable cost thereby making available otherwise unobtainable information. The use of 'what if' scenarios and sensitivity analyses, and the wide use of statistical techniques on large data bases, facilitate planning greatly.

Unfortunately, the construction industry is conservative. It is very uncommon for construction organisations to employ statistical techniques, especially for producing forecasts, such as those of time and costs; the norm is for single figure predictions to be contained by deterministic methods, eg 'normal' methods of cost planning.

Especially in areas such as accounting, in which many techniques and requirements are common across organisations and industries, much computer software is available to produce the required information automatically. Generally, such processing is well known as it has been practised by hand for some time and the processes involved are reasonably straight-forward.

Interpreting

Whilst interpretation of information for decision making is a managerial function, often it is necessary for initial interpretations of input information, data, of results of processing, etc, to be required in order that the information output from the sub-system is intelligible to and comprehensible by those who will use it (a communication activity). Especially if the information or data are in specialist forms, such as the results of statistical tests, eg the confidence intervals of a cost forecast, interpretation by appropriate specialists will be necessary to assist full and accurate understanding of those results.

Thus interpretation is a function of a person's expertise, education and experience in the topic – it is the ability to explain the meaning, validity, applicability and shortfalls of the information to those with less knowledge of that particular subject (at 95% confidence, a cost forecast will be exceeded once in twenty occasions). The function is of particular importance in an industry such as construction where many managers are generalists of highly practical bent, and have attained their position through personal effort and attributes from a trade base rather than via a path of formal education and training for management.

Summarising

The essence of summarising is the extraction of salient points from lengthy information which contains other, subsidiary items. Those salient points must be communicated succinctly to those who need the information. A sound knowledge of the subject matter and of the managers' (who need the information) requirements are invaluable in producing good summaries, eg published summaries and comments upon leading legal cases affecting construction organisations.

A summary must be clear, concise and communicated well. The summary should not exceed two pages of A4 size with typing 1½ to double-spacing; a couple of appendices or diagrams in addition may help to expand items of particular importance. 'Type' must be clear and free from errors – so checking and editing are vital. Precise language and good writing style are necessary and presentation must focus the recipient's attention on the most important elements 'at a glance'; list formats, underlining, italics, etc, are helpful techniques. Use short sentences and provide the content of the summary in a hierarchical form, starting with the most important item. Don't waste words; active statements are shorter (and more dynamic) than their passive counterparts.

Communicating

Figure 5.2 depicts the process of communicating. Although the model indicates a single sender and a single receiver, both may be multiple, eg *Multiple senders*: choir; football crowd. *Multiple receivers*: theatre audience; people who pass a building site.

The sender decides what message she or he wishes to send and then encodes that message. Encoding is the process of putting the message into transmittable form – speech, writing, pictures, etc. For long/complex messages, a combination of forms may be used. In deciding the form(s), the sender should consider:

(a) the message – nature, complexity, length
(b) abilities of the sender, and
(c) requirements and abilities of the recipients.

Some communications forms may not be available, eg brain-wave transmission; television. 'Noise' considerations, feedback and experience, and knowledge/information of effectiveness and appropriateness will help in determining the most suitable forms of encoding and transmission.

Often the communications medium and the transmission channel are regarded as synonymous. Although their differentiation may be important in some cases (medium is general, channel is a particular facet of the medium), it is not vital here. Considerations (a) to (c), above, are applicable to the choice of the medium and channel for transmission.

As communication is a two (or more) party process, it is essential that the recipient be evaluated, and his/her requirements (consider the provisions of JCT 80 regarding variations). A recipient undertakes three primary functions in the communication process: *reception*, *decoding* and *understanding*. No matter what medium and channel is used or how well the sender has satisfied the requirements of good communication, the receiver's reception will not be 100%. Transient media, eg speech, and lack of repetition or reinforcement of the message reduce the level of reception (and/or retention of the message). Decoding should be straightforward via use of a common language, clear terms, diagrams, etc; unfortunately often this is not the case due to 'noise' factors – ambiguity, imprecision, jargon, etc.

KOONTZ *et al.* (1984) indicate the recipient's final stage to be understanding the message. Unfortunately the understanding will be restricted and so the third process of the recipient is described better as perception of the message, ie the recipient's impression/

belief of what the message is intended to convey – which may be different from what it states, and both may be different from what the sender desired.

Factors which detract from efficient communication are termed *noise* (some have been noted above). Noise may be *internal to the parties* – imprecise language, jargon, poor concentration; *internal to the sub-system* – inappropriate channel, intermediary is able to put own interpretation on message thereby introducing errors which go uncorrected; or *environmental* – weather conditions affecting television broadcast and reception as well as the people involved.

It is very helpful if a feedback loop can be introduced which provides a facility for checking the efficiency of the communications. Naturally, as feedback itself will be a communication sub-system, the sender's assessments of the sub-system actually is of the primary system *and* the feedback loop. Hence, the loop should be kept as rapid, as short and as simple as possible, eg a client briefs an architect and then inspects the primary drawings and specifications produced.

Apart from the noise components considered above, various other factors may occur to reduce the efficiency of a communication:

Sender's distortion/omission – sender delivers a message which is incomplete or designed to produce a particular result; not a lie but a version of the truth (see chapter 2 *Politics* page 35).

Receiver's perceptual bias – receiver hears-perceives what the receiver desires or is ready to hear; unwelcome news may be distorted or disregarded. Emotional overtones may distort the reception of information; body language plays a vital role in face-to-face communications, and voice tones are important.

Untrusting – lack of trust between participants produces 'screening'/censorship of communications.

Format 'hierarchy' – non verbal communications tend to obliterate verbal ones; written communictions, eg books, carry more weight than verbal communications, eg lectures, communication to a general audience (public) may have more 'clout' attached to it than communication to a closed audience.

Status – especially relative status is highly influential – people are far more willing to accept information from an 'authoritative' source; reputation and known qualifications are important factors.

Immediacy – the more immediate (obviously requiring urgent action) drive out the less – helpful in keeping up to date but reduces background knowledge; can be a problem in construction which has the aura of 'fire brigade management'.

Distance – physical/communication stages and intermediaries – is inversely proportional to effective communication; reduces clarity and introduces much potential for, or actual, noise.

Overload – too much information causes severe clouding – difficult to detect and retain salient factors.

Conflict – when people are in conflict or are antagonistic towards each other they tend to withhold information or to distort it in communications. This may occur also in power hierarchies, especially when people are seeking more power. Information is gathered and secreted rather than shared, the result is a breakdown in communications.

Often it is the case that a breakdown in communications is the initial manifestation of more basic problems; a communications breakdown is the first stage in a progression of dispute/conflict which may end in arbitration or, ultimately, litigation, eg disagreement over a variation – time and money entitlement of the contractor.

HANDY (1985) suggests three main principles to foster efficient communications and to help overcome potential problems.

(*a*) *Use more than one 'communications net'.*

  (i)   hierarchical

                    formal

  (ii)   expert group

  (iii) status group

                   informal

  (iv) friendship group

Use of informal nets before using formal nets has been found to improve recipients' levels of retention of information communicated – the communications are received from more than one source, and on at least two occasions, and so reinforcing occurs.

(*b*) *Foster two way communications.* Although two way communications can be rather time-consuming, this approach does improve both comprehension and retention of the messages.

(*c*) *Ensure that the communications chain is as short as possible.* Shortening the chain reduces the possibilities of distortions and errors caused by intermediate communications; direct communications should be the most efficient.

Communications occur both internally to the organisation, eg cost-value reconciliation, and externally, eg Interim Certificate. By communications with its environment, an organisation becomes an open system enabling it to interact with the environment and respond to environmental changes – an important factor for construction organisations in obtaining orders and for procuring productive resources.

Recently much attention has been devoted to developing effective communication techniques. Most are inter-active, computer based methods in which the computer system poses questions to the user, who then responds; by this iterative approach, results of decisions are simulated – expert systems are of this form. A new mechanism of extended scope has been developed by a research team under Professor JAMES POWELL. It employs a video disc to supplement the computer system and has produced a package to educate people about fire in buildings. A key component is that the user is able to simulate what that person would do in the instance of being involved in a fire. The 'package' demonstrates that by personalising the simulation through interaction, realistic portrayal of situations and use of visual and verbal communications, the messages are conveyed efficiently.

5.5 Outputs

The outputs of the sub-system are various types of information. Often the primary information will be supported by 'appendices' of supplementary information and, sometimes, data. The outputs are *historic*, a record of what has happened; *snapshot*, a statement of an instantaneous situation; *forecast*, a statement of what is expected to occur in the future.

The purpose of the information sub-system is to service other systems within the organisation. In providing that service it is helpful to recall that information which does not contribute to the success of an organisation is not necessary – it is an element of waste. An important part of the information sub-system is the technologies which are employed to assist people in producing, handling and communicating the information. All too frequently organisations obtain the latest, complex and, often, expensive technologies to process data – this can be counter-productive and loss making as the technology can swamp the intended users and purposes. They key is to select technology which is appropriate; especially in small organisations, computers may not be warranted and performing tasks by hand remains the most efficient approach.

Information provides visibility. A company's annual report and accounts depict the success of that company's activities over the year in financial terms. It is helpful if the sub-system provides regular information, in agreed and constant formats, on activities which management seeks to and, given the information, should be able to control, ie affect performance. Constant formats facilitate comparisons, trend analyses, etc. Agreed formats assist use of the information by managers, eg monthly cost-value reconciliations.

Even if the information itself is not a forecast, it should be structured so as to enable managers to use it proactively, ie to predict. Such information will be a primary component of managers' early warning mechanism for detecting actual or potential problems and hence prevention of the problems' occurrences or growth. Thus, the outputs of the information sub-system should be decision oriented; this will affect the choices of both the inputs and the conversion processes.

Information must be timely. Information which is available too late for management to take effective action upon it is redundant. Thus the more rapid production is, the more frequently information is required and the shorter must be the lag between the data collection and information provision. For example, information about the properties of a batch of concrete, particularly its strength, is more helpful before the concrete is placed than after it is cured and supporting other components of the building – if the concrete is inadequate, the remedial actions in the two cases will differ vastly.

By providing visibility, information assists in the delegation of authority; properly structured information will show who is responsible for what. The use of cost or profit centre accounting systems provide such visibility. A matrix approach to project management information, as illustrated in figure 5.4, is suited to construction organisations. It is useful for the information sub-system matrix to accord with the management system matrix. The project information sub-system will show project performances, as required by the project managers, and resource input needs, as required by the function managers.

In addition to providing information to project and function managers, the sub-system must provide information to customers,

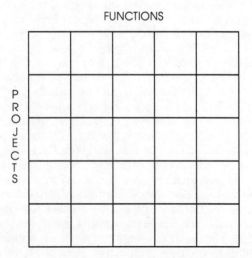

5.4   Project Management Information System (PMIS) matrix

owners and statutory bodies as well as the top managers and/or directors who manage the whole organisation. The information required by statutory bodies is formal and tends to be a requirement which changes only occasionally and, usually, at predetermined times, eg the passing of a new Act. However, the sub-system needs to be flexible to enable it to meet the needs of individual managers and to be adaptable to both a variety of projects/activities and to customers' and others' requirements.

As construction is a project-based industry, information sub-systems may be viewed as networks:

Local Area network (*LAN*) has access points on, and provides information about, a single project.
Wide Area Network (*WAN*) covers several projects.
Value Added Network (*VAN*) incorporates storage, processing, etc.

Computers provide great scope for information networking. A VAN which incorporates all the organisation's projects is very useful in achieving control.

Control is required in three categories of managerial functions:

(a) *Operational control* concerns everyday activities, routine operations such as payroll. *Transaction processing sub-systems* (*TPS*) are used, the information outputs of which do not yield information for other areas of managerial action (but may be integrated into another category which does).

(b) *Management control* involves short term planning which requires an *information provision sub-system* (IPS) which outputs routine and ad hoc summaries and reports produced from detailed data handled by a TPS, eg sales trend analyses.

(c) *Strategic control* is long term. *Decision support sub-systems* (DSS) help by providing answers to 'what if' questions. By predicting the outcomes of alternative courses of action, rational decision making is aided. The sub-systems employ forecasting models which are bases on heuristics ('Rules of thumb') and probabilities to give the outputs.

Expert sub-systems are valuable aids in supplying ready access to specialist knowledge via a computer-housed facility. The sub-systems operate by requesting the user to input answers to series of quite clear and simple but highly pertinent questions which the sub-systems displays on the computer screen. The sub-system uses the answers provided in a set of progressive decisions and elimina-tions alternatives (via heuristics and probabilities) to arrive at a conclusion. This 'expert opinion' output is obtained readily and rapidly but is as flexible only as is the system.

Perhaps the major facet of information is that 'information gives power' [HANDY (1985) page 243]; who controls the information, controls the operation. Control of information through restrictions on access, confidentiality, etc, protects the territories and objectives of people and is extremely important in setting out hierarchies. Rules and regulations are used to restrict information flows and access, these are particularly prevalent in bureaucracies. It is quite common for informal contacts to be established with the main purpose of overcoming the restrictions and thereby gaining access to the information.

Information distortion is a problem which, by its very nature, cannot be measured. It occurs unwittingly through incorrect use of information, such as by deciding to invest in new plant based solely on cost comparisons and so ignoring the benefits side of the equation. More ominously, distortion occurs through misuse of control over information, a common example is a project surveyor's hiding profit/income on valuation reports produced during the early stages of a project in the belief that the activities executed later will be less profitable – the action enables the surveyor to smooth the profit profile of the project (for discussion of this distortion see FELLOWS (1982)).

Formality of outputs
Outputs span the spectrum of formality from very formal statutory requirements for information, eg annual accounts requirements in accordance with the provisions of the Companies Acts, to totally informal opinions expressed in casual conversations. The credence which should be given to information will depend, inter alia, on the formality of its issue and communication channel and the status of the person(s) providing and conveying the information.

Informal information is a means by which information provided formally may be modified. At a company's Annual General Meeting the shareholders will have received copies of the annual accounts and directors report; formal speeches and questioning are employed to provide/obtain further information, however, informal personal discussions after the meeting frequently yield very valuable information. Personal contact, especially where the informality provides a degree of anonymity for the source(s) of information, can produce invaluable supplements to, and explanations of, formal information. 'Off the record' statements often are the most revealing but, because of their nature, ethical use of them is limited. Some of the information will not be a product of an organisation's information sub-system but will be 'grapevine' information or pure speculative personal opinion. Despite its rather dubious character, such 'information' gives helpful 'background' and 'colouring' to assist in understanding a situation, behaviour, etc. Compare the effects on a contractor's bidding for a project of two contrasting rumours about the client:

(a)   the client is about to embark upon a major programme of expansion which will involve much new building work;
(b)   the client is short of funds and may be forced into liquidation in the near future.

It is in the interests of an organisation to control information, especially that which flows out from the organisation and so may be gathered by investors or competitors. Thus, information which leaves an organisation tends to be formal.

Historic information

Historic information records what has happened. On its own it is of very little value. However, series of historic information can be used to detect trends, eg trends in turnover from profit and loss accounts, and so form an input to forecasting. Further, by using historic information of what did occur and comparing those results with what had been planned, variances and the reasons for them can be detected. Such variance analyses form a very important (and widely used) means of formulating corrective action provided, of course, that the information is available in a timely way. (Information which shows performance on an operation to be poor can be used as a basis for correcting the performance only if the operation is still being executed.)

Much information regarding performance achieved can be provided as exception information which highlights areas where actual performance differs from what was planned. The exceptions show areas for action by management. One common assumption is that the planned performance is correct, eg a construction programme; an estimate; a cash flow forecast. This assumption is extremely dubious. Plans are predictions and, as such, contain variabilities if not errors. Thus, a manager should determine that the exception actually exists (comparison of like with like is being made), that the plan is still applicable (conditions have not changed materially – is clay being excavated instead of sand?) and that the exception is real and not just within the plan's margin of variability. If those conditions are satisfied, a true exception exists and remedial action is required.

Snapshot information

Snapshot information rarely concerns the future, usually it records a moment in the past, eg a Bank Statement, or states a current situation, eg a label on a new box of screws which describes the contents. Snapshot information is a statement which applies either momentarily (as for a Bank Statement of an organisation) or for a, usually short, period (as the label on the box of screws and the commencement of its use).

Especially that snapshot information which is used in labelling is communicated in formal and standard ways. This is of great assistance to users who thereby know where to find particular items 'at a glance'.

Some snapshot information occurs as the result of evaluations of historic information – a cost value reconciliation compares costs incurred and revenues receivable up to a given instant but the result of the evaluation of the two sets of historic information is a snapshot of the project's profit at the instant under examination.

Forecasts

Good forecasts are essential to good management. Only by determining accurately what the future holds and the consequences of actions which the organisation may take can the best courses of actions be selected. Other things being equal (which they are not) the organisation which produces the most appropriate and most accurate forecasts and then, logically, makes the best decisions and takes the most suitable actions will be the most successful.

As forecasts are predictions they contain inherent variability due, inter alia, to the inputs and forecasting techniques used. The objectives should be to:

(a) know the size of forecasts' variabilities, eg standard deviations, and

(b) reduce the variabilities to be as small as possible, within 'sensible' costs of producing the forecasts.

Aim for forecasts which are accurate, unbiased and efficient.

Construction programmes, resource requirements, eg materials requisitions, estimates and tenders are examples of forecasts made everyday by construction organisations. Further, it should be recognised that clients briefs to designers and their designs as expressed in drawings, specifications and, to some extent, bills of quantities (which are snapshots also) are forecasts of what building is required. It is not very surprising that variations receive much attention.

5.6 Feedback

Feedback is vital; it is the mechanism by which the sub-system can be monitored and so changed to improve its performance.

The feedback loop incorporates information concerning the outputs of the sub-system as provided to the users – adequacy of outputs, accuracy of outputs, timing of outputs, communication mechanisms, and so on. The feedback system should be an auditing process to ensure that information provided which is not used (is redundant) is omitted in the future and that information which is needed but not provided is introduced. The process should also evaluate the ways of providing information, levels of detail, distribution etc.

Caution is necessary regarding, 'it would be nice if', and analogous statements concerning provision of additional information and retention of existing provisions. Only useful information is required. The acid test which must pervade any effective feedback (auditing) process is, 'does the value generated by the (increment of) information at least cover the costs of providing that information?'

Questions

1 (a) Explain the role of feedback within management information systems.
   (b) Analyse the uses and benefits to be derived from feedback concerning:
        (i)   the performance of directly employed labour
        (ii) the performance of sub-contractors
        (iii) the profitability of projects.
                                    CIOB *Building Management II* 1987

2 Analyse the causes of poor communication in the building industry between designers and constructors and examine the effects of these upon site productivity.
                                    CIOB *Building Management II* 1988

3 Many building companies are providing computer facilities on site with the object of improving the quality of information available to site management.
   (a) Discuss the extent to which recent developments in information technology have made this objective attainable.
   (b) Assess the benefits that may be expected to accrue to building companies from the introduction of computer facilities on their sites.
   (c) Identify those areas of site management activity likely to be most affected by these developments.
                                    CIOB *Building Management II* 1986

4 A building company's head office may be considered to be at the centre of its communication network.
   (a) Describe the primary function of the office in relation to the communication process.
   (b) Comment on the significance, in this context, of recent developments in information technology.
                                    CIOB *Building Management I* 1986

6 The Social System

6.1 Introduction

Again this chapter uses a systems approach to explore the social system which operates within building organisations. This system will be the plasma in which the social relations of the organisation are contained and using our systems description, we can identify the Primary Task of the social system as being: to ensure that the work of the people within the organisation is carried out effectively and meets employees aspirations.

The systems model which will be used to develop this chapter is shown in figure 6.1. As can be seen there are three inputs to the system. The primary one is the central resource, people. Secondary inputs will be the industrial culture within which they work and the patterns of education and training which they bring to their work. These then are the raw stock which are converted by the system process into the outputs. The conversion processes will include the way in which such people are motivated, the way in which they are grouped, how they are led and the quality of the communications within the system. This conversion process leads to some outputs. These have been classified as a social product with satisfied, committed and involved personnel along with the product of group working which underpins much construction activity.

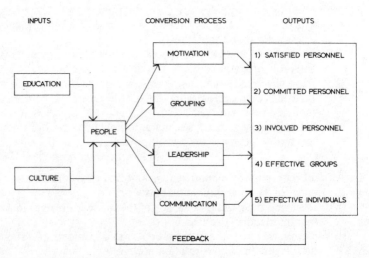

6.1 A systems model of the social system

The output will of course feedback into the inputs because the products of the conversion will shape the nature of people coming into the system and the culture and skills they bring with them. Finally the system boundary needs to be identified and for the purposes of this chapter the social system boundary is that which is included in the directly employed sector of the building organisation. Whilst others, such as sub-contractors, suppliers, design teams, etc, will all impact the inputs to the system, for the purposes of analysis in this chapter, they are deemed to be outside the social system boundary.

6.2 Inputs

The nature of people

There are varying assumptions about the behaviour of people. These assumptions make up a *'Weldenschaft'* – a world view which shapes our personal standards and outlook. Inevitably the assumptions we hold shape social relations and managerial relationships in a work setting. Such assumptions are often selected in the kind of phrases we may use. The following phrases starkly illustrate some contrasting positions – they are not real but they can illustrate some differences.

'Building workers are bone idle these days – the only way to get them to work is to pay 50p an hour more than the site down the road'. Such phrases suggest that the person holding such views regards human kind, and building workers in particular, as lazy and may only be motivated by economic interest. This view was expounded by FREDERICK TAYLOR in the early part of the twentieth century. Another view could be expressed by *'Just leave them alone, they know what they are doing and they'll do a good job'*. This alternative view suggests that people in organisations are positive and self motivated, they work hard for the satisfaction of a job well done. Indeed management researchers such as DOUGLAS MCGREGOR have long argued that jobs should be designed to enable the worker to obtain self expression.

A third view could be summed up in a phrase such as *'Now if I had Surinder on the site he'd do a good job – the conditions are just right for him'*. This illustrates the contingency approach where the person, the style, the setting combine together to produce good results.

These three crude illustrations serve only to demonstrate different approaches but are these managerial attitudes formed by the individual, independent of outside forces? or are they shaped by the social and environmental process? Underlying this question are two long standing debates, the first that of *Nature* v *Nurture* and the second, of *Free-will* v *Determinism*. For the purposes of this chapter the question could be *'Are managers born or are they made?'*

Those who say that managers are born would hold to the view that the genetics, heredity and instincts which Nature gave us, shape our behaviour and that we have little control over them, eg the idea that instincts drive us all and a Manager (or subordinate) may be 'instinctively aggressive', by 'instinct cautious' or 'rash', etc. This has been 'refined' by a group gathered under a general title of *'Sociobiologists'*. This controversial creed argues that peoples' behaviour is dominated by a desire to preserve their genes and that evolution breeds in (or out) certain behaviour.

A similarly deterministic approach is taken by those who believe that personality is the dominant force in behaviour. Psychodynamic theories argue that personality and temperament are determined by events in the first five years of life. Trait theorists are less deterministic but argue that these enduring aspects of the personality are difficult to change and will hold over a number of situations. So an extrovert manager at work is likely to exhibit these traits in all settings.

In contrast to these positions, those who support the Nurture and Free-Will sides of the debate, view the individual as being shaped not by inheritance or early life so much as by what is happening in the here and now, and that more recent events are far more influential in shaping behaviour. This responsiveness to the situation will mean, if the environmentalists are correct, that people are more flexible to the situation and can demonstrate a range of styles and behaviour dependent on the situation.

The synthesis of these arguments is the cognitive approach to behaviour. This approach puts the individual between the environment and the behavioural response. In this theory the individual interprets the environment and this interpretation is based upon the skills, limitations, memory etc of the individual. The behaviour is based upon the world as perceived not necessarily as it is. Thus, the given behaviour is a response to the environment filtered through the personality and predelictions of the individual.

To summarise, some three behavioural models can be observed:

1 Internally generated behaviour
2 Environmentally generated behaviour
3 Behaviour generated by the environment but modified by the individual.

A small example can illustrate the differences. A firm is having difficulty with absenteeism on a site and decides to institute an attendance bonus. If a worker shows up for five consecutive days in the week he gets a £10 attendance bonus.

Harry, turns up every day and keeps getting his bonus. The analysis of this phenomena would vary. The internal behaviour person may analyse it as Harry being a stickler for time keeping. The bonus is irrelevant to his behaviour. The environmentalists would argue that the bonus *of itself* is shaping Harry's attendance record.

The cognition theorists would note the bonus and note that Harry expects to get the bonus and that the £10 is attractive to Harry and so plays a part in encouraging Harry to turn up to work.

All the theories predict the same outcome but explain it in a different way.

However, the social system does not only rely upon a psychological analysis of the inputs. Social processes will also be important in shaping the character of the inputs. In particular culture, especially an industrial sub-culture of the building industry, will shape the behaviour of people within the social system. REIMER (1979) investigated the cultural aspects of working in the American construction industry. In his book *Hard-hats* he uses an anthropological approach to analyse work behaviour of construction workers. It is perhaps predictable that REIMER (op cit) confirmed many of the commonly held perceptions of the American building worker; aggressive, frequently a misogenist, and wedded to a culture based upon 'machismo'. Such a culture would intervene in the way building workers are managed for if the management style does not naturally fit with the prevailing culture then it is not likely to be successful. This is not to argue that tough, aggressive management is likely to be more effective than a consultative pattern but that values and attitudes have to be taken into account when the 'conversion process' of the social system is undertaken.

Finally the inputs will be shaped by instrumental factors such as education and training. This will be an important factor within the social system since it assists in forming and constantly reinforcing the cultural norms of the building industry. Indeed one purpose of training is to inculcate the sense of shared values of the building industry. There is frequently a training sub-system within building organisations and this will intervene into the social system of the organisation. It is not the intention of this chapter to address the training sub-system.

Human beings who share a common industrial culture and similar training are the stock of personnel which the Manager in a construction organisation has to work. Most theorists accept that the working environment is influential upon people's behaviour and the skilful Construction Manager must seek to manage the environment in order to maximise the potential production output from those around him. This manipulation of the environment not only refers to the physical setting but also the social setting of work. The social setting of work is controllable by the processes of management, therefore the conversion processes associated with the systems model are likely to include the following:

  - how the employees are motivated
  - how the employees are grouped
  - how they are led
  - how well the communication process works.

6.3 The Conversion Processes

Motivation

How well a Construction Manager motivates people at work will be an important factor in influencing their performance, and the social system is important in providing the framework for this contract. It should be noted that motivation is only one of the factors influencing performance and classical studies have seen performance expressed by the equation:

Performance = f (Ability, Motivation)

This classical equation has more recently been added to by a third factor – 'role perception' – this is concerned with the expectations of what one is supposed to do; knowing what to do as well as working hard and ably at what you are doing.

If the equation holds true then we can improve performance by changing the ability by more training or the motivation under which these activities are exercised. If motivation is shaped by the environment then changing the motivation may be seen as an easier route to better performances than changing the individuals traits. However, this analysis needs to be refined, improving performance is not merely a question of pulling levers to rectify the environment. The task itself, the individual *and* the environment in which these come together are likely to influence performance. This synthesis has developed over time and has been the product of theorists over the last sixty years. It would be useful to describe the growth of the 'science' of motivation for the questions which face us are as pertinent today as they were in the early part of the century. Questions such as: Why do people work? What motivates people? can be used as a framework for analysis.

This review does not address the essential practical aspects of motivation. The theories are useful in attempting to explain the underlying systems of what people do, but do little to explore the question 'How do we motivate people?' Often the answer to this question lies in the structure of rewards which people are given for improved performance. It is important to note that different people have different needs and desires, and a reward system which reflects different aspirations is more likely to be effective than unitary systems. Firstly, people will work hard for something they value. Secondly, motivation increases when objectives are clear. If someone has a known performance target when the person is more likely to be motivated to achieve it. The task of setting standards of performance is not, of course, simple. It presumes that 'good performance' can be prescribed and for many repetitive tasks in a stable environment this may be so, but in construction with a variable environment and fragmented tasks then performance is less easy to define. Even harder is the task of defining 'good performance' in managerial work where much of the work may be based upon group effort, committees and a highly interdependent environment. The essential control in this type of setting is well thought out appraisal schemes where goals can be set and joint evaluation of the progress towards these goals can be made.

Thirdly, the rewards for good performance, and the penalties for poor or non-performance, must be known and accepted. Most motivational theories accept these factors but differ in the weight given to each. In order to compare each theory it is useful to describe briefly the origins and essential features of each theory.

Motivation theory
There are broadly three categories of opinion, firstly, that man always works out of sheer necessity, as a means to an economic well-being, secondly, that he works in order to satisfy his social needs for human relationships, and thirdly that he works in order, ultimately, to satisfy higher order social and psychological needs, in particular the need for self-fulfilment. One writer on motivation, SCHEIN (1965) has classified these in a characterisation of management assumptions about the nature of people. They are *Rational-economic man*; *Social man*; and *Self actualising* man.

Some may argue that the division is artificial and that the classifications are not a matter of either/or but a combination of all three with different saliences being placed on different approaches at different times.

Notwithstanding the basic divisions of opinion as to the reasons why men work are, to a large extent, reflected by the historical progression in thoughts about motivation. The idea of work as mere economic necessity is very much the traditional one and the majority of the earlier industrial organisations were structured accordingly.

In recent years, however, the influence of behavioural scientists has been present through a much greater emphasis on the social and psychological aspects of organisation, which in turn tended to slacken the rigidity of traditional ideas.

Although in hindsight the management efforts to induce their employees to produce more were in effect motivating them, management did not seem to recognise motivation as a concept. In order to trace this progression of motivation the work of certain theorists will now be analysed as having been vital as the stepping stones of motivational development.

FREDERICK TAYLOR

From the first recorded social histories of slavery and serfdom up to the 1930s labour was largely considered to be a commodity and an expendable one at that, which could be bought and sold in the market place. In the sixteenth century 'homework' predominated and in the industrial revolution payment by 'piecework' was normal. Any kind of measurement aimed at determining what the piece-work rates should be was apparently completely absent.

FREDERICK TAYLOR, an American engineer was one of the first empirical researchers in industrial psychology to apply scientific methods to the study of man. His 'scientific management' techniques introduced in about 1880 attempted to measure tasks and improve efficiency. No one questioned the efficiency limits of workers and therefore there was no scale by which to ensure that a worker was giving his all for his employer. He considered that careful analysis of a job would allow a far greater advance in efficiency.

The traditional approach to motivation as developed during this era rested on the fundamental philosophy that the cost effective means of motivating workers was through a direct relationship between rewards (or penalties) and performance. The rewards or incentives would take the form of promotion, conditions, shorter hours and so on, but would most often be money in the form of higher wages.

It is on such a principle that the operation of functional incentive schemes is based. The underlying assumptions of scientific management and in turn of incentive schemes about human nature and motivation have been summarised by MCGREGOR (1960) in what he calls the *Theory X approach* to management. These are that:

(a)   The average human being has an inherent dislike of work and will avoid it if he can.

(b)   Because of this human characteristic of dislike of work, most people must be coerced, controlled, directed, threatened with punishment to get them to put forth adequate effort toward the achievement of organisational objectives.

(c)   The average human being prefers to be directed, wishes to avoid responsibility, has relatively little ambition, wants security above all.

The system is therefore one of external control, which is based on the allocation of rewards and punishments in accordance with predetermined standards.

As suggested by VROOM and DECI (1973), in their introduction to a series of writings about motivation, this approach is a reflection of what psychologists refer to as the 'law of effect and the principle of reinforcement', which states that where a person undertakes an action which is followed by a reward, it is highly probable that the action will be repeated, ie the carrot and the stick.

As the scientific management approach gained popularity, the number of reported problems associated with employee morale, turnover and absenteeism increased. Managers, in their quest for profits, began modifying the basic system as jobs became more efficient, by putting severe constraints on the incentive system and thereby limiting workers' income. Simultaneously, fear of job security arose. As workers became more efficient, fewer were needed and redundancies became commonplace. Workers responded by restricting their output in an attempt to optimise their income, while at the same time protecting their jobs.

Despite the admission of TAYLOR and the abandonment of the theory by other industries some of the principles of scientific management are still practised in construction. Operatives are paid basic wages and bonus as on top of this. Such wages structure conforms to the underlying principles of scientific management. However, incentive schemes envisioned by TAYLOR cannot have said to have been a success in construction, different sites with different production situations with unrealistically set targets leading to frustration or bonanza's and friction between trades could hardly be called 'scientific'. Moreover the variability of production conditions can vary the output dramatically. FORBES (1969) showed that bricklayers required between 600–1900 hours to build identical dwellings. TALBOT (1976) has shown that whilst economic man may behave differently if given a pay rise that it is not a durable incentive. In short, if a building worker is bored with his job more pay will not make it less boring. It may be easier to tolerate for a short time but any underlying cause of dissatisfaction remains. Nonetheless the construction process with its variety and range of social contacts has avoided the most dehumanising aspects and Taylorism and the industry is left with the rump of scientific management – its payment structure.

Following TAYLOR's 'Scientific Management' the focus of research moved to studying the worker not the work and the Human Relations School was developed.

ELTON MAYO
During the late 1920s and early 1930s MAYO had been called in to run a large series of research projects into industrial conditions at the Hawthorne plant of Western Electrical in Chicago. Some of his projects were into the existing group and intergroup structures, others were into better working conditions. The trigger to the main turning point after TAYLOR was in his experiment on lighting conditions in the telephone relay assembly room. During experiments, as luminosity was raised so production increased. It was raised again, and production increased. It was then decreased to the

level of moonlight and production still went up. Obviously external factors must have been influencing the results and it was the study of these external factors that set the tone of the era. MAYO then looked at the social interaction of the group rather than their lighting conditions. As MILLER and FORM (1961) comment of the experiments:

'They show there is something far more important than hours, wages or physical conditions of work, something which increases output no matter what was done about physical conditions.'

At the end of the various experiments, following changes in personnel, conditions of working, etc, it was found that:

(a) workers tend to develop group attitudes, norms and values so they react to management not as individuals but as members of groups

(b) the physical ability of workers is of little significance in comparison with 'social ability' in determining the amount of work to be carried out

(c) non-economic rewards have a significant role to play in motivating workers. It was discovered that social factors were playing a significant part in determining productivity. Workers were not producing as much as they were reasonably physically capable of, but were producing amounts which were socially acceptable to the group involved in carrying out the work. It appeared that men were setting their own acceptable norms for a 'fair day's work' and those who produced more became socially outcast. This meant that there was considerable social pressure to group members to conform to group norms.

The significant conclusion of these experiments is that:

'None of the results, gave the slightest substantiation to the theory that the worker is primarily motivated by economic interest. The evidence indicated that the efficacy of a wage incentive is so dependent on its relation to other factors that it is impossible to separate it out as a thing in itself having an independent effect.' (ROETHLESBERGER and DICKSON (1945))

In other words the human relation theories were totally opposed to the findings of TAYLOR. MAYO (1949) himself discounted the incentive of money by stating that:

'. . . man's desire to be continuously associated with his fellows is a strong, if not the strongest human characteristic.'

In later years much investigation has been carried out into these classical studies and doubt has been cast on the naivety of examination leading to conclusions that were perhaps required rather than discovered. Many observers considered that there was too strong an emphasis on social satisfaction at the expense of any influence that the economic needs of individuals may have on behaviour. It is possible that workers may actively seek to satisfy both needs through the social controls over output and earnings. More specifically, this is achieved by their manipulation of incentive schemes as an attempt to effect their ideas of a fair day's work. This would appear to be in tune with MARCH and SIMON's (1961) philosophy of 'satisficing', whereby the worker is working as hard as is necessary to achieve an acceptable level of earnings.

The human relations view challenges many of the assumptions about the management of labour in construction. Its movement away from pure economic interest clash with the trends in payment structures with much more of the labour force being involved in labour-only sub-contracting with its emphasis upon the material benefits from work. However, it is noticeable that construction work is almost invariably carried out in gangs or groups. These work groups are the primary production force and how they establish 'a fair days work' is part of the groups ethos, as is the development of a group ethos with gang leaders who act as spokesmen for the group to the site manager.

The next stage in development was the 'needs' theory introduced by ABRAHAM MASLOW and being developed by McGREGOR and HERZBERG.

ABRAHAM MASLOW

The orderly development of the broad physiological and psychological need classification theory was first put forward by MASLOW in 1943, although its use has only really been applied to industry since being popularised by McGREGOR (op cit). Based on clinical observations, MASLOW identified five sets of goals which he termed as 'basic needs' which if largely unsatisfied, tend to produce tensions in the individual. The needs suggested are:

(a)   physiological needs, such as food, sleep, shelter and sex
(b)   safety needs of security and protection
(c)   love needs of association, affection and belonging
(d)   esteem needs of ego, self-confidence, status and reputation
(e)   the need for self-actualisation.

The fundamentals of this theory rests on two main principles: First, that hierarchy is one of importance. If a man is hungry and thirsty he will have scant regard for anything else and when these physiological needs have been satisfied he will then be more concerned to obtain shelter, security and other 'safety needs'. He will continue to seek to satisfy his 'higher needs' for esteem and self actualisation. Second, to use MASLOW's words, 'a want that is satisfied is no longer a want' (1966). People are dominated and their behaviour organised by an unsatisfied need, eg if hunger is satisfied it becomes unimportant to the individual at that time. The hierarchy of needs is illustrated in figure 6.2. MASLOW's theory, although often criticised as too simplistic in that a hierarchy may not exist or will be present in a different order for different groups or individuals, has nonetheless been the basis of much motivational investigation by psychologists. McGREGOR added additional insights on the satisfaction of man's needs as a means of motivation. Building from the assumptions that satisfaction of a lower-level need is no longer a source of motivation he concluded that traditional management techniques were not effective motivators. By providing good wages, good working conditions, excellent fringe benefits and continuous employment, management has satisfied the lower physiological and security needs and shifted the emphasis to higher needs. A worker will now be motivated when he can satisfy these higher needs and will be frustrated if he cannot satisfy them. Traditional management approaches that emphasise direction and control through wages and job security are bound to be ineffective; they concentrate on the lower needs that are already satisfied, while ignoring the higher needs. From this analysis McGREGOR developed his *Theory Y approach* to management. He assumed that:

(a)   the expenditure of physical and mental effort in work is as natural as play or rest

(b)   external control and the threat of punishment are not the only means for bringing about effort towards organisational objectives. Man will exercise self-direction and self-control in the service of objectives to which he is committed

(c)   commitment to objectives is a function of the rewards associated with their achievement

(d)   the average human being learns, under proper conditions, not only to accept but to seek responsibility

(e)   the capacity to exercise a relatively high degree of imagination, ingenuity and creativity in the solution of organisational problems is widely, not narrowly, distributed in the population

(f)   under the conditions of modern industrial life, the intellectual potentialities of the average human being are partially utilised.

If MASLOW's theories are acceptable to management, then the implications are obvious, for it then becomes the manager's responsibility for creating an organisational climate in which employees can develop their full potential. This would involve providing opportunities for increased autonomy, greater job variety and responsibility in order to satisfy the employees' higher order needs. Failure by management to provide such a climate will result in a frustrated, alienated and unfulfilled work force, leading

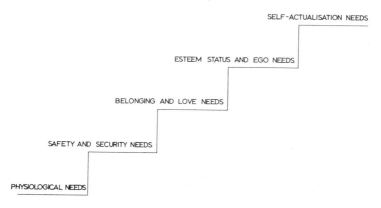

SELF-ACTUALISATION NEEDS

ESTEEM STATUS AND EGO NEEDS

BELONGING AND LOVE NEEDS

SAFETY AND SECURITY NEEDS

PHYSIOLOGICAL NEEDS

6.2 MASLOW's needs hierarchy

to lower job satisfaction and poorer performances on the part of the individual. The study of needs was further developed by HERZBERG in studies which indicated that MASLOW had only tackled half the problem.

HERZBERG's major work *The Motivation to Work* (1957) shows a systematic and realistic approach to analysing the main motivators. His initial study was of some two hundred engineers and accountants employed by eleven firms in the Pittsburgh area of the USA. He asked his subjects to:

(a) describe specific incidents in their recent experience which had made them, feel either particularly good or particularly bad about their jobs

(b) what effects these incidents had on their subsequent attitudes and performance

(c) whether these effects were of short or long term duration.

Analysis of the results indicated that the two separate sets of factors were at work in causing worker satisfaction and dissatisfaction. He found that the only way to motivate the employee is giving him challenging work in which he can assume responsibility. Most schemes fail because the satisfaction provided is not inherent in the work. The worker simply produces enough to maintain his job; satisfaction results from trading wages, extra spare time, etc, for higher level satisfaction. Other distinct separate factors, those that satisfy lower level needs, are involved in job dissatisfaction. The five factors that have the strongest influence on job satisfaction are achievement, recognition (for achievement), the work itself, responsibility and advancement. Major factors that caused dissatisfaction were company policy and administration, supervision salary, interpersonal relations and working conditions. It appears that the factors that caused dissatisfaction were mainly important

negative way; they were important in their absence, or if they were unsatisfied and for some reason HERZBERG called them *hygiene factors*. They could have the effect of reducing a person's motivation if they were not satisfied, but they could not increase a person's motivation. The real motivators were those at the top of MASLOW's hierarchy, the 'higher needs'. These theories were developed and 'job enrichment' suggested as a means of motivation. Figure 6.3 illustrates HERZBERG's two factor model and figure 6.4 shows a comparison of the MASLOW and HERZBERG models.

In the construction industry one major element forever present is the need for employment. Hiring and firing is still rife in the construction industry but investigation has shown that much is brought about by operatives not wishing to relocate with the next job. SHENFIELD (1968) found that 60% of those interviewed were not prepared to live away from home, and PHELPS BROWN's (1968) studies indicated 67%. The security aspects have also proved important in studies by THOMAS (1963) where 21% of those studied said that if they left the industry it would be to find a steady job, and CARNEGIE (1975) who found that 70% of those interviewed felt they could derive a sense of security by having a trade. The absence of security for building workers may have a detrimental effect on productivity. As BAYLEY (1973) notes:

> 'while at any particular point in time these needs may be satisfied, and in consequence no longer motivate a person to achieve anything about the acceptable norm, should you deprive or even threaten them, trouble will ensue. Start talking of redundancy, or even see yourself becoming redundant by virtue of the project, or your stage on it, reaching its conclusion and the thoughts are automatically directed away from the job in hand to the search for security elsewhere. productivity automatically drops'.

On examination of the higher needs one can see that these are not usually well catered for although elements of satisfaction may be found in the nature of the work itself. Additionally many operatives fulfil their desires to become a member of a group by making serious efforts to work with their friends and form cliques on site. Experiments both in the UK and US have shown an increase in output where men are allowed to choose those they worked with.

The ego needs can, to an extent, be satisfied by the job content. Construction work is not particularly repetitive, it is usually done in the fresh air and offers some sort of direct challenge. Because of the nature of construction most tasks create opportunities for a person to use his personal skill and initiative to do a job well and thereby provide the motivating factors of achievement, recognition and responsibility. Too often, however, this status will be in the eyes of the workmates and not often by management. The esteem and status needs are also only really catered for from within the industry

6.3 HERZBERG'S motivational model. From The Motivation to Work, *F Herzberg, Wiley 1957*

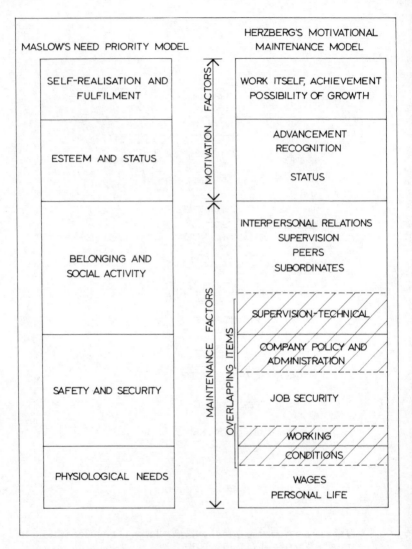

6.4   Comparison of MASLOW'S and HERZBERG'S motivation model

itself for the general reputation and standing of the building industry is not high. This general viewpoint was found by PHELPS BROWN (op cit) in the 1960s and is still present in the 1980s. Much will need to be done for the construction worker's lot by all employers and other bodies in the professions before the public image changes.

Self-fulfilment or self-actualisation is the need to realise one's potential. These needs paradoxically are potentially the most satisfied of all the operatives' needs in the work situation. SAMUEL (1971) records:

'When one considers the final sequence in MASLOW's hierarchy, one reached a poignant paradox. . . . The paradox is that although the "lower" levels of the hierarchy have not been attained in construction in general, the constancy of the technology, particularly in building the close integration of men, materials and tools into meaningful tasks suggests potentially greater scope for satisfaction of this need than in perhaps almost any other industry.'

The archetype construction craftsman or labourer is still considered to be a rugged individualist, willing to take some risks, ready to work and produce with his hands. He will derive much self-fulfilment from working on a physical, tangible task with satisfaction from performing the work itself. Many managers on large sites have failed to appreciate the higher needs of operatives. Too often poor planning, lack of materials, bad bonusing, etc, have combined to frustrate the operative in his attempts to do good work.

The theories of McGregor can also be found in the construction environment. Often head office staff delegate almost all responsibilities to the site supervision. Site agents desire, however, to regulate their foremen and they, in turn, the operatives, thus withholding much responsibility from the men on the site. Theory Y may well apply in the upper levels of decision making, but Theory X is too often applied lower down. Although site agents may believe that operatives will try 'to get away with as much as possible' when unsupervised, research both in the UK and US has shown this not necessarily to be the case. In the UK both NEALE (1981) and SYKES (1969) cite situations where men have worked well whilst unsupervised particularly if a more relaxed Theory Y approach has been applied giving them more control of their task.

In the US BORCHERDING and OGLESBY (1974 and 1975) have undertaken investigations with construction craftsmen concluding that if the operatives could decide how to tackle a task the output was increased. Their studies also considered job satisfaction and job dissatisfaction. They found job satisfactions to be 'complete a task, good workmanship, productive day, physical structure and social work conditions'. Their research into satisfaction factors was broken down into that felt by project managers, superintendents (site managers), foremen, tradesmen and apprentices. Although the emphasis and wording changes, typical comments were as follows:

'Satisfaction comes from starting with nothing and ending with a complete project;
Watching things progress, moving a job on schedule;
Signing my name to a job that I did was very satisfying.'

This relationship of productivity causing satisfaction is the inverse of the results they expected, where satisfactions effect productivity and can be an effective motivator. This, they claim, illustrates HERZBERG's theory that workers can be motivated by satisfying higher level needs through work itself. The operative finds satisfaction in a productive job because it allows him to satisfy self-fulfilment needs through his good workmanship and productive output. The consideration of dissatisfaction was equally supportive of their view and generally non-productive jobs, limiting output had the effect of not satisfying higher order needs. One comment by one worker summed up their findings:

'It isn't uncommon for me to spend half the day scrounging around the site for 5 or 10 cent items. Under these circumstances I cannot get much work done in a day; whereas, if the material is available, I feel satisfied when I put in a hard day's work and get a bit accomplished.' (BORCHERDING and OGLESBY 1974)

The majority of studies within construction to practically apply motivational theories have been based upon need satisfactions. SCHRADER (1973) in particular has attempted to give practical methods by which construction managers may motive their work force. These have been supported by HAZELTINE (1976) in the US and MASON (1978) in the UK. There is little doubt that the recommendations made by SCHRADER will have something to interest most operatives. They are:

1   introduction to firm
2   information for operatives
3   family tours
4   trading stamps as bonus
5   methods improvement
6   praise and
7   get the men involved.

There is little evidence to suggest however that such schemes have been widely applied to construction, or that they are flexible in that operatives have different needs.

EDWARD LAWLER and LYMAN PORTER
LAWLER and PORTER followed up both HERZBERG (op cit) and BRAYFIELD and CROCKETT's (1943) earlier studies with regard to the correlation of performance to satisfaction. Although earlier

MASLOW (1956) had suggested that the two were linked with performance being dependent on satisfaction BRAYFIELD and CROCKETT found:

'There is little evidence in the available literature that employee attitudes . . . bear any simple . . . . or appreciable relationship to performance on the job.'

Both surveys did find more consistent evidence for relationships in the expected directions between job satisfaction and turnover and absenteeism. As MASON (1978) has argued the progression of human relations thinking has advanced from believing that satisfaction leads to performance; to the satisfaction/performance relationship being moderated by a number of variables; to performance leading to satisfaction. LAWLER and PORTER (1968) developed this last view.

'Good performance may lead to rewards which, in turn lead to satisfaction, this formulation would say that satisfaction, rather than causing performances as was previously assumed, is caused by it.'

The LAWLER and PORTER model (see figure 6.5) arranges the ten variables involved in the satisfaction/performance relationship. The most important aspect to this study is the factors that affect the effort. LAWLER (1973) later simplified the equation suggesting that the effort expended by an individual is based on the following principles:

(a)   The individual's motivation to perform a particular task is determined by his assessment of that task rather than his general state of well-being. That is, he is concerned about future events rather than those of the present or past.

(b)   In his first assessment of the task he tries to assess what level of performance he may achieve for a given amount of skill and effort. In other words, he tries to determine whether he can do what is required of him.

(c)   He then assesses what the results of this successful performance will be.

(d)   Finally he evaluates the attractiveness of these results.

The effect of the first principle requires managers to look to the future in order to achieve specific objectives regardless of history, a manager will still require to motivate his work force to achieve the next given task. Given a construction example, the form of incentive scheme operated in the later stages of the Thames Barrier contract offered additional bonuses for completing specific and

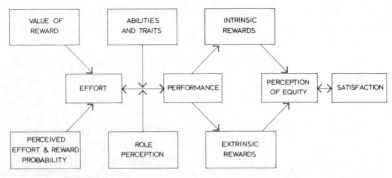

6.5   PORTER and LAWLER's *satisfaction performance model*

easily identifiable stages of the project on or before a specified date, regardless of previous performance. The above principles are often categorised as the expectancy: valency approach due to the two assessments made by the operative, ie what are my expectations of a successful outcome and what is my valuation of the consequent rewards.

Grouping the people
'Not another meeting' must be one of the most frequently voiced observations in organisations. Because the building industry is organised by amalgamating the efforts of many different organisations the number of meetings and groups that managers and professionals are involved in is likely to be greater than many. But if such work is so intolerable then why do we spend so much time working with other people in groups? Building managers can spend up to half their working day in groups of one kind or another and the more senior the position the more varied and extensive is the contact with groups.

So, if the building industry is based around the efforts of groups it is a vital managerial task to group people appropriately. A building manager in order to manage the social system needs to understand the group process and this will be part of the 'conversion' part of the social system. If managed properly this will give use to an output which will be individual and group effectiveness in the work setting.

1   What are groups?
A group is in some senses self defining – any set of people who see themselves as a group is a group. The expression can vary from the work setting where functional groups form, ie the estimating group or the temporary works design group; it may be project based such that a group is formed for a particular project and disbanded when it is over; it may be managerial in function – the board of

directors or partners of a professional practice. Finally in a work setting it may be ad-hoc such as task force to investigate certain technical aspects of a project. But these examples are all drawn from the work setting where groups may be formally established. Naturally we have membership of social groups within the setting of work which may overlap with formal work centred groups. Examples here could be the Friday lunch time Pig and Whistle group.

But it must be stressed that a group is not merely a collection of individuals. For individuals to form a group there must be a distinct objective which is common to the members of the group. In the examples given earlier the temporary works design group has the obvious objective of designing temporary works and this is recognised and *accepted* by group members. Equally, the Pig and Whistle lunch time group is only a group in as much as the members have a common objective of meeting at a certain place at a certain time with a loosely defined membership criteria, ie they are all employed at the same place of work. But there is one overriding qualification in both instances – a group is a group because the members perceive it to be a group. There are obviously other sorts of groups – family groups and groups of friends, but this area is beyond the scope of this book. Groups, then are universal and permanent in building organisations but what do groups do?

We can classify the work of groups into three broad duties:

(i)   *aggregating skills and talents* for the purpose of:
 (a)   distributing work
 (b)   collecting ideas and information for problem solving and decision making.

(ii) *Controlling* by:
 (a)   testing ideas brought before a group
 (b)   delegating the work to the appropriate individuals
 (c)   co-ordinating the work effort.

(iii) *Team building* by:
 (a)   resolving conflicts between individuals or groups.
 (b)   encouraging people to participate in decisions.

The above list will reflect the organisation's need for groups but in order for them to work properly then the participants need to draw some satisfaction from participating in groups. Simply put, individuals have a need to affiliate with others to satisfy social needs – they need to be with others to share something. The objective of this sharing may be based upon the task at work or by gaining help and support which is not directed to the task but is more political in nature. In short, harvesting help to carry out one's own objectives which may or may not match the organisation's objectives. Finally individuals often need to define themselves in relation to others within a group, eg the 'deputy project manager' – the person is defining their role in relation to another in the group.

2 How are groups formed?

Like individuals, groups at work grow over a period of time. HANDY (1976) classified the development of groups in a useful rhyme. He suggested that groups follow four stages of development, namely *forming, storming, norming* and *performing*. Considering these in turn:

(a) *Forming* Here the participants are a set of individuals yet to recognise that they are in the process of forming a group. These early stages are characterised by individuals wishing to make a personal impression upon the putative group. Styles of leadership, duration and title of the group may be the subject of some discussion.

(b) *Storming* This is a turbulent time for most groups and the new group is likely to exhibit a considerable amount of conflict over its objectives, style of leadership and personal ambitions of group members.

(c) *Norming* In this phase the group start to establish norms and practices. Issues such as 'how it should work, what degree of openness, trust and confidence is appropriate' emerge (HANDY 1976). In short, the group members are feeling one another out to see if individual expectations of the group are being matched by other members.

(d) *Performing* At this stage the group has reached a level of maturity which enables it to be productive (although it must be said that the formative stages (i) to (iii) can produce useful work).

This process of growth may take place naturally but performance will be hampered by the pace of the move to maturity. The paradox in construction is that group working in projects is essential yet little time is available to develop this group ethos as the pace of the project frequently outstages that of group development. Some managers in construction have used techniques built around theories of Group Dynamics which help group development. These techniques are centred upon the 'process' of how the group works rather than the task it has been asked to do. In construction, with its emphasis upon practical framework and temporary project teams, it is often worthwhile in spending time in developing a team ethos by participating in exercises which accelerate the development of group formation.

Communications

The communication system of an organisation is at the heart of the social system. The importance of communications within building

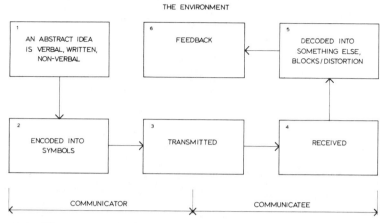

6.6   *The communication process*

organisations is reinforced by the amount of time individuals spend upon communicating. (In construction one may argue that the professions are solely transmitters of information, the architect receives a brief and translates it into drawings to communicate to the builder; the quantity surveyor provides cost information, etc.) It has been estimated that the amount of time dedicated to communication is between 50–90% of the working day. A process so important has generated a great deal of research, but under-pinning this research, has been a generalised model of the communication process. MEGGINSON (1981) represents this communication process as shown in figure 6.6

As can be seen from this model the communication process requires a communicator, a message, a channel of communication, a communicatee and a surrounding environment which sets the context of the communication. One may ask the question why do we need to communicate information; several reasons exist.

1   *Reducing uncertainty*   For example the site manager asks the architect to clarify details or the accuracy of the architect's intentions.

2   *Gathering information*   For example the site manager puts in a 'request for information' document to the architect to check details of an assembly. Equally the architect seeking information about the strength of the concrete poured may be an example of this kind of information.

3   *Confirming preconceptions*   Here the communicator is looking for confirmation of a view already formed. The estimator may ask a colleague about the job which he is bidding. Is it going to go for

£10½m? – what do you think? The communication is intended to serve as support to a belief already held.

4 *Influencing events*   For instance at a site meeting communications are put forward which do not offer or request information but the communicator feels the need to influence the course of the meeting. Those holding certain positions in the organisation may be 'expected' to communicate more than others. Moreover the site manager may be, because of his status relative to other members of the site team, prepared to influence events to a greater degree than others and consequently communicates more frequently. The different types of communicators say little about the effectiveness of communications within construction organisations. In general, reinforcement of the message by mixing the means of communication enhances the effectiveness of the communication. As the numbers of media used to communicate grows then the chances of a message being received increases. So if we speak and write a message it has a greater chance of being received, understood and acted upon. The medium of the message is not the only factor influencing effectiveness. The more layers that a message has to go through the more likely its informational power will be lost – if a message goes through five levels in the organisation then it may lose up to 80% of its informational content.

If construction organisations need to improve communications then there are certain techniques which can be introduced. A list of do's could look like:

(a)   In written communications, use appropriate styles of writing and appropriate lengths of communication. (For example the 400 page report is unlikely to be read by the site manager – a two page summary may be.)

(b)   Establish credibility for the written communication – the message must be understood and believed. Messages may confirm facts or seek action. The fact confirming message validates information. The 'action' message instructs the receiver to do something.

(c)   In verbal communication skills are needed to speak and communicate with the voice. The way we say things is as important as what we say.

(d)   Listening is also vital and can be learned as a management skill.

Leadership

Leadership is a key managerial process in the social system of a construction organisation. The management of sites or businesses depends upon the leadership qualities and the type of leadership exercised by those responsible.

From this it follows that one of the key organisational tasks is to recruit, train and retain people with leadership skills. But what are leadership skills? Are they inherent in the person or dependent of the actions taken by the person. In short, is leadership dependent on personality or behaviour? To answer these questions it is useful to break down the study of leadership into two parts, viz:

(i)   What are the personal or behavioural characteristics of leaders?
(ii) What makes leaders effective?

There are several approaches to answer the first question. Leadership may be studied in a number of ways. The following list identifies different approaches to understanding leadership:

- trait approach
- behaviour approach
- functional approach.

1   The trait approach
This way of looking at leadership has the longest history. The underlying theory is that the reason for certain people becoming leaders was related to their personal characteristics. Early work focused upon 'great men' to study if there were any common characteristics or traits which could then be used to identify future 'great' leaders.

The results of these studies appeared during the 1940s and 1950s and the results were disappointing to the theorists for little correlation between traits exhibited by leaders could be found. Even more, some studies found positive correlation whilst others were negatively correlated. Later work by STODHILL (1974) is more encouraging to the trait approach the notes in a review of the literature that in fifteen studies of trait leadership:

(a)   the average person who occupies a position of leadership exceeds the average member of the group in the following respects: (1) Intelligence; (2) scholarship; (3) dependability in exercising responsibilities; (4) activity and social participation; (5) socio-economic status

(b)   the qualities, characteristics and skills required in a leader are determined to a large extent by the demands of the situation in which he is to function as a leader.

STODHILL goes on to say that:

'the average person who occupies a position of leadership exceeds the average member of his group to some degree in the following respects: (1) sociability; (2) initiative; (3) persistence; (4) knowing how to get things done; (5) self-confidence; (6) alerts to, and insights into, situations; (7) co-operativeness; (8) popularity; (9) adaptability and (10) verbal facility.'

So the current thinking is that the trait approach is helpful in some ways but that one needs to look at the *situation* on which these traits were exercised.

2 Behaviour approach

If traits could not fully explain why leaders became leaders the question was re-focused upon studying what leaders actually did. Work carried out by BALES and SLATER (1955), FLIESHMAN (1973) and KATZ and KAHN (1979) seemed to identify two different styles, one was related to the task in hand, the other based around interpersonal relations with those being led. So we can identify two contrasting styles:

task – centred leadership
people – centred leadership.

The comprehensive literature review by STODHILL (op cit) revealed that there was little difference in the productivity attained if different styles were used but that *style* made a major difference to the satisfaction experienced by those who were being led. The third dimension of leadership studies is the *functions* that leaders perform and a study of *what* leaders do independently of the way they do the job may be revealing.

The functional approach

The functional approach considers leadership to be an analogous of three functions:

- defining the task (procedural functions)
- achieving the task (substantive functions)
- maintaining the social cohesion of group (maintenance functions).

It would seem that it is difficult to find leaders who are good at all of these functions since they require different orientations – the first two depending upon task centred leadership whilst the last one requiring a more people centred leader. In this circumstance leadership is often split between two persons who can complement one another. In construction the site manager and general foreman often 'do a double act'; one being very task orientated, the other being more concerned with the emotional maintenance of the personnel on the site through the application of good interpersonal skills.

This then gives three approaches to leadership behaviour, but the second question 'what makes a leader effective?' is still unanswered. The foregoing has suggested that effective leadership was dependent upon the right person being in the right place at the right time. This theory of leadership gets at the heart of effective leadership behaviour. It was pioneered by FIEDLER (1967) and suggests that in order to be effective a leader's 'style' must be matched to the situation. This is called 'a contingency approach to leadership'. This general banner covers a range of theories about effectiveness of leadership. It is useful to classify these:

    (a)   FIEDLER's contingency theory
    (b)   goal theory
    (c)   adaptive-reactive model.

FIEDLER's theory

FIEDLER (1967) has argued that leadership is a metaphor for influence – the degree to which a leader can influence group members behaviour is seen as important to the understanding of leadership. Moreover this 'influence' was manipulated in three ways:

   (i)   The quality of the relationships between the leader and the led (where relations are good the leader has more influence than when the relationship is poor).
   (ii) The nature of the task. If the job is 'structured' then it is easier for the leader to tell the led what to do.
  (iii) The position of power of the leader. If the leader can decide on rewards or punishments then he or she is likely to have greater influence.

These three dimensions constituted the 'situation' in which the leader found him or herself. By combining them in the manner shown in table 6.1 some eight situations could be described.

Leader-Member relations	Task structure	Position power	Rank order of how favourable the situation is
Good	Structured	High	1
Good	Structured	Low	2
Good	Unstructured	High	3
Good	Unstructured	Low	4
Bad	Structured	High	5
Bad	Structured	Low	6
Bad	Unstructured	High	7
Bad	Unstructured	Low	8

Table 6.1   International leadership

So eight situations are defined. The next step is to measure the leader's orientation – is he or she a task orientated person or people orientated. FIEDLER used a measure called *Least Preferred Co-worker Scale (LPC scale)*. This instrument asked leaders to recall the person who they had least enjoyed working with and then describe them on a set of scales. A favourable description of the least preferred co-worker indicated a people orientation, an unfavourable description suggested a task orientated leader.

These two factors, the 'orientation' and the 'situation' are then put together. The results of FIEDLER's work are shown in figure 6.7.

It shows that the task orientated leader performs better in very easy or very difficult situations but in moderate situations a person orientated leader appears to be the most effective.

Path – goal theory
The theoretical underpinning for this theory is drawn from the expectancy theory of motivation discussed earlier in this chapter. In essence it draws into the picture of leadership effectiveness the role of the 'follower' with the task at hand. The leader's behaviour is seen to shape the follower's perception of whether a *goal* (or target) can be achieved. Also the *paths* which need to be taken can be made easier or more difficult by the leader's behaviour to the led, ie the leader can bestow or withhold rewards (either physical or inter-personal) to the led to make the achievement of the subordinate's goal more or less easy. For example, a gang of concretors are given a 'job and finish' task. Clearly the men want to finish as fast as possible to enable them to leave early and the gang think they can finish by lunchtime. The target of a long liquid lunch is attractive to the gang but in order to achieve it they need some equipment. The site manager can make it easy by providing the equipment or difficult by not doing so. In this way the leader (the site manager) is influencing the outcome experienced by the gang. However, the explanation must be melded with the type of persons in the gang. Some of the gang may have 'an internal locus of control' ie they believe that what happens to them is a function of their own behaviour. Others may have an 'external locus of control', ie those who believe that they have little influence upon what happens to them, its all a matter of luck. From studies by MALE it would appear that those persons with an internal locus of control prefer a participative, people centred, leadership and those with an external locus of control are satisfied with a directive, task centred leader. Is the effectiveness of the leadership as dependent on the match between the leader's style and the personality of the led? But what about the task? Tasks which are familiar to those doing them will require a more person centred approach. Whilst an unstructured, unfamiliar task will benefit from a more task centred style.

Returning to our concrete gang, it is likely that a directive leadership style would not be effective if the gang are doing something with which they are very familiar, say laying concrete in slabs. Here a supportive and encouraging style is likely to be more effective than constant reminders of what to do and how to do it. However, if the same gang have to place concrete using a tremmie tube and no-one in the gang has experience of this method then

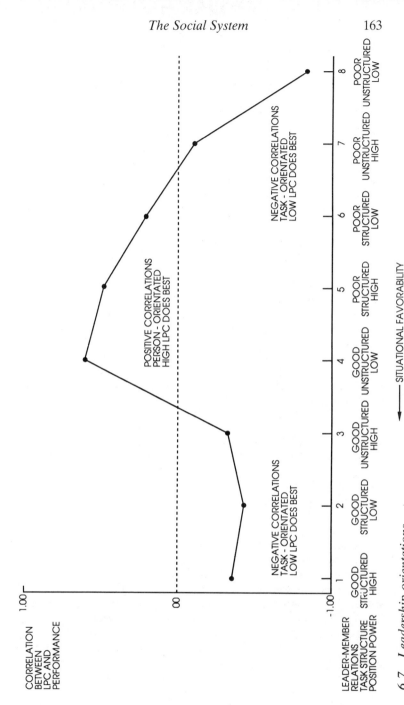

6.7 *Leadership orientations*

advice on structuring the job (how to do it) and what to do would be welcome to the gang.

So the path-goal theory enables us to predict the leadership style most effective given certain conditions and certain types of subordinate. It is the match of the situation, the subordinates and the leadership style which is required to encourage leadership effectiveness.

The adaptive-reactive model

This theory is again based upon the contingency model but focuses upon one of two frameworks for the study of leadership effectiveness. They are:

1 the organisation in which the leader works; and
2 the quality of social encounters experienced at work.

The common bond is that the leader, to be effective, must *adapt* to the organisational setting, eg a drill sergeant is unlikely to be effective in a university setting, and that the leader must *react* to the expectations of subordinates. The leader must adapt to the organisation in which he or she works. The organisation is shaped by its size, its complexity, the corporate culture and the type of technology used. Leaders in complex organisations where relationships are formal and the culture is disciplinarian are more likely to be successful when adopting an autocratic approach. So the leader's style is shaped by the organisation.

The reactive approach depends upon the relationship between the leader and the led. It postulates that leadership is not based around a coherent style but is dependent upon the leader's relationship with the individual sub-ordinate and that different styles are used with different people. This would suggest that the leader and the led come to agree about their expected behaviour. The implications of this is that leaders do not have a natural style which is 'lowered' on to subordinates but that leadership is shaped by the environment in which it is exercised as much as shaping the environment.

The implications of these theories of leadership are evident. The person selected for leadership positions within the company will need to match the specifics of the job. For example because someone is a good site manager it does not automatically mean that he or she will perform well as a contracts manager; the job, the environment and the people are different. The contingency approach seeks to set different leaders in control at different stages of a project or a company's growth. For example a site manager who is an entrepreneur may be best suited to set up a project, a person with sound administrative skills may be better placed to manage it through the middle and end phases. So management orientations may need to match job needs. In some cases the tough hard-nosed approach is necessary, in others a more relationship orientated approach is found to be better suited to the situation. In a study of construction project managers BRESNEN *et al.* (1986) found that there was a strong association between good performance, as measured by adherence to programme, and relationship orientated project managers. This connection was stronger on longer and larger contracts suggesting that if time is allowed for a relationship orientation to develop then it pays dividends. This finding stands in stark contrast with the self-perception for site managers to be 'production' orientated. This is reinforced by the emphasis given to the 'tasks' in recruitment, selection and training processes.

6.4 Outputs

The model postulated in figure 6.1 sought to show that the product of managing the conversion process was five-fold; employees who were:

- satisfied
- committed
- involved
- displaying group effectiveness
- individual effectiveness.

Job satisfaction

Staff who experience greater job satisfaction are likely to have done so because they find that they are working with considerate and friendly colleagues and are in a challenging job which has been clearly defined which is equitably paid. The consequences for the firm is that employees are healthier (mentally and physically), have less time off work and have a lower staff turnover.

However, it must be noted that recent studies have only found a weak correlation between job satisfaction and productivity. Indeed the reverse has been argued – that high productivity causes satisfaction. But employees with job satisfaction create the setting for a smooth running, supportive organisation.

Commitment

By handling the management processes effectively it is likely that employees will develop commitment to the organisation. This is the state of loyalty and identification with the policies and culture of an organisation. Those personnel with high commitment have a greater desire to achieve the organisational goals and tend to remain in organisations which provide jobs which offer 'responsible' jobs.

Involvement
Involvement is different from commitment. Involved employees
tend to think deeply about their job and the job provides the
dimension of the persons status. Involvement tends to be expressed
by employees who have autonomy in other jobs (typically site
managers), a variety of tasks (anyone in the industry) and be able to
participate in decision making. The products of involvement are
similar to commitment in that they are not directly related to
necessary input but more associated with the contextual issues of
organisational life; lower turnover, punctuality in meeting dead-
lines and a willingness to work long hours.

   The outputs of job satisfaction are focused upon the 'soft' issues
not increasing productivity. But these 'soft' issues, absenteeism,
turnover, etc, cost construction companies many thousands of
pounds each year – this is of itself a rationale for seeking the outputs
described. Secondly the identification of dissatisfaction of
employees can assist in directing the organisation to attend, with
more vigour, to the management processes discussed in the
'conversion process' section of this chapter.

Effective groups
We can see that groups need to be managed if effective performance
is to be obtained and this will be a system output. But how are
groups best managed? Several factors are involved in getting a
construction related group to perform effectively. They are:

Group size
Here there is a paradox. The larger the group the greater its
constituent skills but the more cumbersome to handle and for group
members to feel a sense of belonging. Conventional wisdom
suggested that groups of around five to seven are the optimum but
this must be accepted as a crude measure.

The task of the group
Clearly the size of the group will need to relate to the task it has to
perform. For example collecting information about construction
techniques used for hospital buildings can draw upon either a small
or a large group – the process of collecting and disseminating the
information can allow a larger group than say resolving a specific
technical detailing problem. For problem solving or generating
ideas smaller groups tend to be effective. Also the criteria for
effectiveness needs to be considered. Is the task urgent or
continuous? Does the task demand high precision or a cheap
solution? As ever the triad of objectives of time, cost and quality are
in constant tension; groups need to reflect upon the task and the
criteria for success. As with most tasks the clearer the objective the

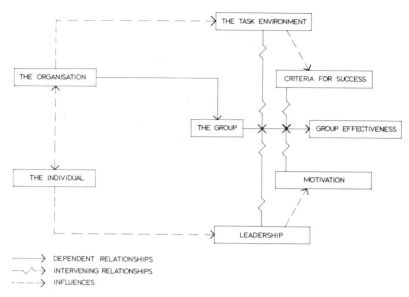

6.8   Group effectiveness.

easier the task and the more likely it is to be successful. Further, the more important the task to the individual group member then the more committed the person will be to the group.

Interspersed factors within the group
Other factors such as leadership style, and motivation will also intervene to shape the effectiveness of group performance. Figure 6.8 shows a model of the relationships between some of the factors influencing group effectiveness.

When discussing task performance it might be thought that the tasks expected of groups would be undertaken in a dry, perhaps automatic way with a strong emphasis on 'doing'. Groups have *tasks* to perform in order to achieve objectives but there will also be processes needed for sustaining the group. Regrettably construction work is frequently dominated by the *task* and the processes of groups is sometimes forgotten. We can separate these processes into two headings:

1   task processes
2   maintenance processes
   HANDY (op cit) lists six activities which groups have to do to achieve the task:

   – initiating
   – information seeking
   – diagnosing

 - opinion seeking
 - evaluating
 - decision-making.

As can be seen all of these are very specific and relate to a sense of order, a continuum of activities for the group leading up to decisions.

But to make a group effective construction managers need to maintain its momentum and cohesiveness. People in groups need encouraging or calming down, etc. The maintenance processes can be listed thus:

 - encouraging
 - compromising
 - peace-keeping
 - clarifying and summarising
 - setting standards.

These processes must be on-going throughout the life of the group and may be seen as setting the 'tone' of the group.

To get the most out of groups construction managers need to provide the surrounding structure of leadership and motivation. Added to these management there needs to be personal skills applied. For example, communications skills which include effective speaking, writing and telephoning are all vital but even more so is the central skill of effective listening. Reading 'body-language' can also be an elusive but revealing science.

Finally motivation systems must rely on participation in decisions which effect people's work. Acceptance of the goals is essential to gain commitment to them. It is the communication process which is vital to the level of motivation experienced by people within the firm.

Effective individuals

Finally the social system will need to produce effective individuals as one of its main outputs. By managing the conversion processes the construction manager is likely to develop the knowledge base and skills of those working around him or her.

6.5 Feedback

In the sub-system as set up in this chapter there will be a feedback loop so that the inputs to the system are informed by the outputs of the conversion processes.

Questions

1 Discuss the contention that job satisfaction is a stronger motivating force than remuneration.

CIOB Part 1 *Building Management I* 1986

2 The motivations of individuals are often modified when the individual becomes a member of a group.

   (a)   Discuss the differences which are likely to occur between individual and group motivation

   (10)

   (b)   Explain why it is important for a site manager to understand these differences.

   (10)

CIOB Part I *Building Management I* (resit) 1986

3 It has been stated that there are two possible relationships between job satisfaction and worker performance:

   (i)   that satisfaction leads to performance;

   (ii)   that performance leads to satisfaction.

Comment upon these statements when applied to production work on a building site.

CIOB Part II *Building Management II* paper 1 1988

4 It is more fruitful to consider leadership as a complex inter-relationship of the manager, the subordinate and the situation rather than the property of an individual.

Discuss this statement in relation to

   EITHER (a)   a building site manager

   OR (b)   a specialist department manager.

CIOB Part II *Building Management II* Paper 1 1988

7 The Management System

The management system is shown in the model in figure 1.4 to be at the centre of the systems which comprise a building organisation. That position is symbolic of its central role in integrating and directing the other systems. The *Primary Task* of the management system is *managerial effectiveness* which is defined as:

> The achievement of intended results by managerial action which is appropriate to the circumstances.

7.1 The evolution of management ideas

The interest in the effectiveness of managers originates in the writings of the French engineer HENRI FAYOL who, in 1916, defined the functions of the manager and propounded the revolutionary idea that management could and should be taught. Eighty years later, his analysis still forms the basis of the most frequently adopted views of management, so much that it is often called the *Classical* school of thought. As with other disciplines, such as psychology, there have been a number of 'schools of thought' in the main stream of the evolution of thinking about management.

The *Great Man* school consists of the biographical and autobiographical literature on managers. This literature contains a wealth of details and anecdotes, but little general theory about managerial work.

The *Entrepreneurship* school is based in the writings of traditional economists who consider that, faced with the need to make a decision, the manager acts 'rationally' in his/her own self-interest – he simply maximises profit.

A related and more recent school of thought is the *Decision Theory* school, which concentrates on the study of the *unprogrammed* decision. To call a decision 'unprogrammed' is to maintain that it is complex and poorly understood, and that the manager can use no pre-determined method in its solution (MINTZBERG 1973). The origin and development of this school lies with HERBERT A SIMON (1976) and his colleagues at Carnegie-Mellon University. This school and the Entrepreneurship school, focus on decision making to the exclusion of all other managerial activities.

Equally the *Leadership* school focuses on leadership to the exclusion of all other activities. The school has evolved historically through three phases. Early research sought to identify the particular *traits* of successful leaders but with little success. Subsequent studies (OHIO STATE, BLAKE and MOUTON (1968) focused their attention on *management styles*, criticising the autocratic, task-orientated style advocated by the Classical school and extolling the virtues of the participative, people-orientated style of management (MCGREGOR 1960, LIKERT 1961, ARGYRIS 1964). A third phase in the evolution of this school has been the rejection of the idea of a 'best' style of managing by a group of researchers arguing for *situational* or *contingency* theories of leadership (FIELDER 1966; CAMPBELL 1970).

The latest school of thought is the *Work Activity* school, which stands at the other extreme from the so-called 'armchair philosophising' of the Classical school in both its approach and findings. The findings of the school are based on systematic research of what managers actually do as opposed to what they should do, using research techniques such as the diary method, activity sampling and structured observation. The work has done much to reveal the *characteristics*, *content* and *contrasts* in managerial work (CARLSON 1951, STEWART 1978, 1976, 1982, MINTZBERG 1973). It has been particularly helpful in recognising the contrasts or differences between managers' jobs within the management system and stands opposed to the universalistic and single dimensional views of some of the earlier schools.

7.2 A systems model of the management system

This brief review of the development of ideas about the management system leads into the input – conversion-output model shown in figure 7.1.

The *inputs* to the management system comprise the *task* or *tasks* which the manager has to complete, the *team* or *teams* with and through which he works on the tasks, and the *manager's* own personality and style of management. The *conversion process* consists of the *functions* or *roles* that the manager pursues in blending the team and the task to achieve the 'intended results'.

The key *outputs* of managerial work are *decisions* about what to do to accomplish the task, the assignment of tasks to enable the team to operate effectively and the provision of support which facilitates performance.

Feedback from performance is monitored against the task, the team and the manager's requirements through a *control* system.

As shown in figure 1.4 the management system operates *within* a context comprising environmental, strategic, structural, informational and social systems and operates *on* the production system.

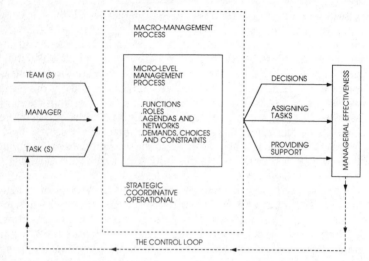

7.1   The management system

The management system receives inputs from each of these systems and exports outputs to each system.

Whilst the conversion process remains constant, different contexts and different inputs will produce different outputs. The essential character of the management system will change as these variables change to create different types of management jobs within the system. Classifications of types of managerial job will be discussed.

To delineate the *boundary* of the management system it is necessary to ask who are managers and who are not? Job labels can prove deceptive – all of those posts with 'manager' in their title may not be management jobs and some posts without a 'manager' label may involve predominantly managerial work. The boundary can be drawn only by the definition of the functions or roles which comprise the conversion process, which will be done later in the chapter. A 'short cut' to establishing the boundary of the management system to consider its outputs. Decisions, demanding actions from others and power to assign tasks are all symptoms of the authority of the manager to direct the actions of subordinates and peers. Those *outside* the management system are therefore the people in the organisation who carry out decisions, receive instructions and use resources. There are boundaries *within* the management system which are traditionally defined by *level* and *function*. In building organisations a further *spatial* dimension must be added to draw the boundary between site and head office based activities. It is important to ensure these internal boundaries don't become barriers.

7.3 Inputs

The inputs to the management system are the task, the team and the manager.

The Task
The tasks of the building organisation are the formally allocated activities together with the informally assumed activities which managers choose to fulfil. Organisations perform multiple, and often conflicting, tasks concurrently (CYERT and MARCH 1963). In building organisations tasks can be defined by *level*, by *function* and by geographical *location*.

(a) Level
It is possible to distinguish three levels of tasks within the management system – the *corporate* level, the *business* level, and the operational or *project* level.

Corporate level tasks are concerned with the direction of the whole organisation and are mainly strategic in nature. The focus is on 'what' the organisation will do. These tasks were discussed in greater depth in chapter 3 but it is worth repeating that these tasks are not self-generated and entail a different and more difficult mode of thinking from the other two levels. We shall review these conceptual skills further when considering the skills that the manager inputs into the system.

These tasks are truly managerial in that they are largely proactive and unprogrammed or non-routine. The 'time span of discretion' is large (JACQUES 1956) and is likely to be in years and months. This is a measure of managerial responsibility developed by JACQUES which notes the duration of time before the manager has to report back to his superior.

A typical corporate level task might be the decision to expand the joinery department which currently services only the company's contracts, to creat a separate, profit centred division to manufacture and market purpose-made and standard products to sell to other building contracting firms.

Business level tasks are tactical in the sense that they are concerned with implementing the strategies detailed at the corporate level. The focus here is on 'how' to carry out the strategy. The tasks are administrative in that they are reactive but they may still be unprogrammed. The time-span of discretion is likely to be in months and weeks. In building organisations these tasks tend to be located at the central or regional offices of the firm. Typical activities would be directing divisional and/or departmental activities which are concerned with a single market or discipline. Typical posts might be Directors of the joinery division or Chief

Surveyor. The Director of the joinery division would be responsible for implementing the strategic decision described earlier which might entail finding workshop space, buying new machines, appointing people, setting up computer systems, preparing a business plan and a marketing plan, etc.

The chief surveyor would be responsible for allocating staff to contracts, providing training in new methods and forms of contract, introducing new computer based systems of cost-control and forecasting, etc. In short, the development of the surveying discipline within the building firm.

Operational or *project* level tasks are specifically focused on short term, temporary objectives. The joinery shop manager will have specific jobs for particular contracts going through the shop at any point in time. The site manager will be co-ordinating the activities of a diverse group of directly employed or sub-contract labour to achieve the completion of the current building project. A significant proportion of the decisions will be technical and programmed with a short time span of discretion, ie days and weeks.

(b) Function

Tasks will vary depending on the function being conducted. In all building organisations basic functions such as getting work, doing work, getting paid and administering these activities have to be performed. In small firms a single individual or two parties may perform all these tasks between them. A feature of growing organisations is the early establishment of specialist functions to get the work (estimating and marketing), to do the work (construction, materials and plant), to ensure payment (surveying and accounting), and to provide supporting services (legal, secretarial and safety). The dividing up of the total work of the organisation is a recognition that different functions require different skills. Comparing two departments, marketing and estimating, which are ostensibly operating in the same area of the business, ie getting work, is instructive.

Marketing is an extrovert gregarious activity involving building up networks of contacts, entertaining clients, etc, and is generally externally orientated. By contrast estimating is largely a solo, insular activity calling for careful and accurate work. The Marketing Director and the Chief Estimator face distinctly different tasks requiring contrasting styles of management.

(c) Location

A feature of building organisations is that they are project based, and therefore some of the key tasks are geographically dispersed to building sites. It is necessary to draw a distinction between central and site or satellite tasks.

At the centre the organisation is primarily concerned with

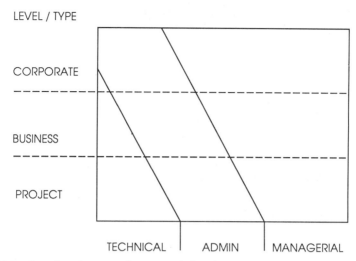

LEVEL / TYPE

CORPORATE

BUSINESS

PROJECT

TECHNICAL   ADMIN   MANAGERIAL

7.2   Level and types of managerial task

obtaining and developing resources to maintain the business. At the site the task is to use the resources to meet the client's objectives. Central activities are largely inward looking, concerned with efficiency and continuity; site activities are outward looking and aimed at effectiveness in meeting the client's objectives with and through a multi-disciplinary team.

The relationship of the levels of management and the types of task is shown in figure 7.2.

The team
The tasks in the building organisation are mainly carried out by teams. These teams can be single or multi-disciplinary and intra- or inter-organisational groups.

Teams *within* the building firm can be formed at project, business and corporate levels. The site manager, for example, may lead a site team, participate in a construction department team, and even occasionally join the corporate team. This last case could arise in respect of a tender for an important contract, where the site manager's advice is valued in assessing the risk factors.

The nature of building project work frequently demands an organisationally separate professional design team and the site manager may also be a member of the project team which is formed *between* organisations and is *outside* the building firm. The formation and development of terms together with teambuilding and managing conflict were covered in chapter 6.

The team is comprised of individuals whose strengths and weaknesses are different and, for a good team, should be complementary. The selection of team members is critical to the success of the business and the project but, particularly in the case of the project, is often outside the control of the manager. Where there is a choice, guidelines have been developed by BELBIN (1981) for creating balanced terms. BELBIN notes the many roles that members can fulfil, and has shown how certain kinds of personality (extravert/introvert, anxious/calm, etc) tend to adopt certain roles consistently. The team roles have been named as follows:

(a) the **Chairman** is the social leader of the group: he clarifies group objectives and sets its agenda

(b) the **Plant**, ie the person with a fluent mind and divergent thinking who creates the new ideas

(c) the **Shaper** who is always looking for patterns in the team's discussion in an effort to unite ideas and push the team towards a decision and action

(d) the **Monitor/Evaluator** with analytical thinking that enables him to assess accurately the feasibility of proposed lines of thinking

(e) the **Company Worker** with a capacity for converting decisions into practical lines of action

(f) the **Resource Investigator** with outside contacts and information, and the ability to stimulate the team and preserve it from stagnation

(g) the **Finisher** who galvanises the team into action and concerns himself with overcoming things that may go wrong or have already gone wrong

(h) the **Team Worker** who offers support and help to individual members and builds up the social character and effectiveness of the group.

BELBIN goes on to suggest five principles for establishing and integrating a management team:

(a) members of a management team can contribute to the team in two distinct roles: their professional role (sales, production, etc) and their team role as described in the above list;

(b) the effectivness of a team will depend on the extent to which its members correctly recognise and adjust themselves to the relative strengths within the team, both in professional roles and in team roles;

(c) each team needs a balance of team roles. The optimum balance will be determined by its objectives;

(d) personal characteristics of individual members fit well for some roles and limit their ability to succeed in others;

(e) only when a team has a balance of team roles, represented by suitable people, can it deploy its technical resources to best advantage.

Another concept which is important to understanding the manager's relationship with the team is that of the *role-set*. As already discussed each manager will be a member of a number of teams and will interact with a range of individuals but the strength of the relationships will vary. By defining the role set of the manager as shown in figure 7.3 the importance of various relationships can be plotted. By inspection the site managers' strongest relationships are with the architect, contracts manager and services engineer and the

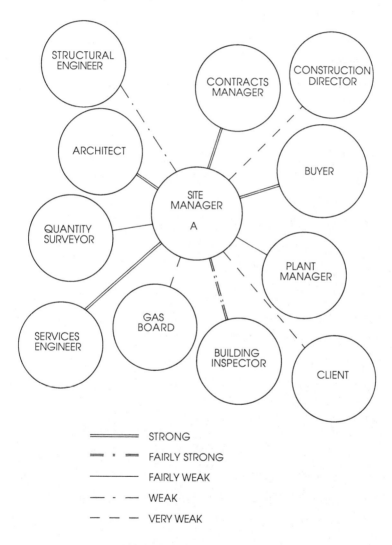

7.3 The role set of a site manager

people with whom he hardly interacts at all are the client, the Gas Board, and his own Construction Director. In addition to identifying key people in the manager's life it may indicate relationships that need to be cultivated, for example, with the Plant Manager.

The manager
The manager himself is an input into the Management System – his skills, knowledge, attitudes and management style will drastically effect the operation of the system.

(a) Skills
One simple classification of managerial skills was suggested by KATZ (1955) who said that effective management rested on three basic skills, each of which could be taught.

(i)   Technical skills
This group inludes the specialist skill and knowledge related to the individual's profession or specialisation. KATZ pointed out that most training programmes were concerned with skills in this area.

(ii)   Human skills
These KATZ defines as 'the executives' ability to work effectively as a group member and to build co-operative effort within the team he leads.

(iii)   Conceptional skills
KATZ saw these as being 'the executives' ability to perceive the significant elements in any situation, and this was achieved through his ability to see the enterprise as a whole. In this way he could see the relationships between various parts of the organisation and their

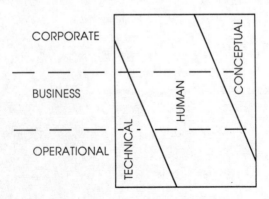

7.4   Skill requirements for levels of management

dependence on one another, recognising that changes in one part effects all others. This is the epitome of the systems approach described in this book.

The importance of these three skills will again depend on the level of the manager within the system as shown in figure 7.4. This diagram relates closely to the types of task shown in figue 7.2.

One skill which KATZ did not list but which has become increasingly, if grudgingly, recognised as a basic requirement for managerial effectiveness is '*political*' skill – in the sense of being able to handle the organisational system.

A useful way of assessing the political skills of managers has been developed by BADDESLEY *et al.* (1987) at the University of Birmingham. They described 'a model containing two dimensions relating, first, to the skills of "reading" the politics of an organisa-

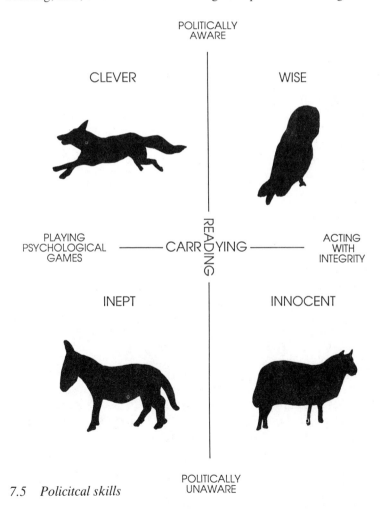

POLITICALLY
AWARE

CLEVER   WISE

PLAYING PSYCHOLOGICAL GAMES —— CARRYING READING —— ACTING WITH INTEGRITY

INEPT   INNOCENT

POLITICALLY
UNAWARE

7.5   *Policitcal skills*

tion and, second, to the skills an individual is "carrying" into situations which may predispose them to act with integrity or play psychological games'. These two dimensions of political skill are given in the model shown in figure 7.5 which allows the identification of four types of behaviour – *innocent* (sheep), *inept* (donkey), *clever* (fox), and *wise* (owl). The important point that BADDESLEY makes is, 'that these behaviours are not fixed traits is a critical distinction, helping us to develop wise behaviour in managers by concentrating in our training on the way the dimensions of "carrying", and "reading" are combined'.

(b)   Knowledge

Managers build up a 'knowledge base' through training and experience which enhances their input to the management system. Traditionally, in the building industry training has been at the craft and technician level and seen as a 'once-in-life' event; recently the concept of Continuing Professional Development has emerged with an emphasis on life-long training. Being able to draw on experience is vital in an industry where every project is unique in total but which has problems the experienced manager is likely to have encountered before. It is regretable that this experience knowledge base is rarely written down and leaves the industry with the individual.

Undoubtedly the complexity of modern buildings calls for knowledge of techniques and information unheard of in earlier eras.

(c)   Attitudes and style of management

A manager's attitudes and values will have a very significant influence on the decisions and actions taken which are one of the key outputs of the management system. No manager is impartial or a model of sound and unbiased judgment. The attitudes revealed at work are likely to influence the effectiveness of the manager to a considerable degree and will be reflected in the management style that is adopted. Style is measured in terms of the degree of people versus task orientation exhibited by a manager. The earlier rather simplistic, assertions of the leadership school of thought that a 'best' style would be identified has been superseded by the more realistic contingency approach of researchers like Fielder whose approach has been applied to the building industry by BRESNEN *et al.* (1985).

7.4 The conversion process

The conversion process within the management system can be viewed at two levels – the *micro* level of the individual manager and the *macro* level of the organisation. The micro level consists of the **Functions** and **Roles** which managers perform.

These are the processes which the system applies to the inputs to produce the outputs. The functions and roles describe what individual managers do – the *content* of the job within the management system.

The functional or roles approaches represent earlier and more recent ways of looking at the manager's job.

The functional approach was proposed by the French engineer HENRI FAYOL over eighty years ago based on his experience of managing a large organisation.

The view that managers perform a set of roles, rather than

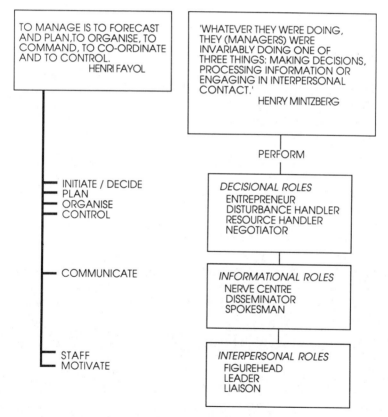

TO MANAGE IS TO FORECAST AND PLAN, TO ORGANISE, TO COMMAND, TO CO-ORDINATE AND TO CONTROL.
HENRI FAYOL

'WHATEVER THEY WERE DOING, THEY (MANAGERS) WERE INVARIABLY DOING ONE OF THREE THINGS: MAKING DECISIONS, PROCESSING INFORMATION OR ENGAGING IN INTERPERSONAL CONTACT.'
HENRY MINTZBERG

PERFORM

INITIATE / DECIDE
PLAN
ORGANISE
CONTROL

DECISIONAL ROLES
ENTREPRENEUR
DISTURBANCE HANDLER
RESOURCE HANDLER
NEGOTIATOR

COMMUNICATE

INFORMATIONAL ROLES
NERVE CENTRE
DISSEMINATOR
SPOKESMAN

STAFF
MOTIVATE

INTERPERSONAL ROLES
FIGUREHEAD
LEADER
LIAISON

7.6 Management functions and roles: a comparison

functions, was proposed by HENRI MINTZBERG (1973) based on his observation of the work of five chief executives. The roles were subsequently confirmed by MINTZBERG and others with a larger and more heterogeneous sample of managers.

The two approaches are often seen as contradictory whereas in fact they are complementary as shown in figure 7.6.

At the macro or organisational level there is, as HALES (1984) points out:

'. . . the need to examine the "managerial" function. The nature of that function within organisations and how it is divided among different managerial jobs is crucially important in defining managerial responsibilities and tasks.'

The nature of the management function *within* organisations is shown in figure 7.7 in terms of level and function. Three levels of management are identified within organisations – *strategic*, *co-ordinative* and *operating* together with functions within these levels.

The conversion process will be discussed firstly in the micro level and secondly at the macro level.

Micro level management process

At the level of the individual manager a number of writers and researchers often, explicitly or implicitly, produce lists of elements which together constitute the *context* of managerial work, even if different managerial jobs display different weightings and combinations of those elements.

Management functions

In modern management theory FAYOL (1916) was the first to propose a description of *management functions*. The FAYOL functions are planning, organising, commanding, co-ordinating and controlling (POC^3 elements). These five functions were defined by FAYOL as:

1 *To forecast and plan*: 'examining the future and drawing up the plan of action.'
2 *To organise*: 'building up the structure, material and human, of the undertaking.'
3 *To command*: 'maintaining activity among the personnel.'
4 *To co-ordinate*: 'binding together, unifying and harmonising all activity and effort.'
5 *To control*: 'seeing that everything occurs in conformity with established rule and expressed command.'

The sequence of the functions is important and logical. An organisation must start with a **plan** – at the corporate level a

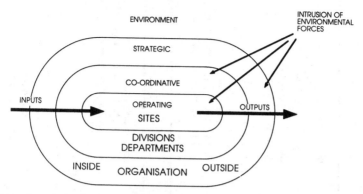

ENVIRONMENT

INTRUSION OF ENVIRONMENTAL FORCES

STRATEGIC

CO-ORDINATIVE

INPUTS

OPERATING

SITES

OUTPUTS

DIVISIONS
DEPARTMENTS

INSIDE   ORGANISATION   OUTSIDE

7.7   Levels in the management system

strategic plan, at the building project level a master programme. It must then design an **organisation** structure to achieve the plan – a *diversification* strategy requires a *divisional* structure (CHANDLER 1966). Third, the organisation must be driven to achieve the plan – **command** must be assumed by the managers. Command refers to the relationship between the manager and his subordinates in accomplishing the task – it is vertical and downward. The site manager will allocate work from the programme to his general foremen. There are a range of organisational activities to be performed which necessitate *co-ordination* between departments, eg estimating and buying and between head office and site. These are horizontal liaison activities. Finally there is **control**, logically the final element which entails checking that the other four elements are performing satisfactorily and specifically completing the cycle by comparing actual with planned performance, eg site progress with programme. The ubiquity of FAYOL's functions has been demonstrated by MINER (1971, 1982) who pointed out that most management text books are organised on the basis of the original classical management functions (including CALVERT's (1970) *Introduction to Building Management*). FAYOL's original five functions have been expanded by a number of writers including GULICK and URWICK (1937) who gave managers one of their early acronyms: POSDCORB. The initials stand for Planning, Organising, Staffing, Directing, Co-ordinating, Reporting and Budgeting.

URWICK has, on other occasions (1943, 1952, 1965) separated forecasting from planning and added communication as another element. Conversely, DAVIS (1951) argues for a telescoping rather than an expansion of the FAYOL's functions into planning, organising and controlling. In his view commanding and co-ordinating are merely phases within the control process.

More recent research by MOHONEY *et al.* (1963, 1965) reported that managerial time can be allocated to a set of eight basic

Role	Description	Identifiable Activities from Study of Chief Executives	Recognition in the Literature
INTERPERSONAL			
Figurehead	Symbolic head; obliged to perform a number of routine duties of a legal or social nature	Cermony, status request, solicitations	Sometimes recognised, but usually only at highest organisational levels
Leader	Responsible for the motivation and activation of subordinates; responsible for staffing, training, and associated duties	Virtually all managerial activities involving subordinates	Most widely recognised of all managerial roles
Liaison	Maintains self-developed network of outside contacts and informers who provide favours and information	Acknowledgements of mail; external board work; other activities involving outsiders	Largely ignored, except for particular empirical studies (SAYLES on lower- and middle-level managers, WHYTE and HOMANS on informal leaders)
INFORMATIONAL			
Monitor	Seeks and receives wide variety of special information (much of it current) to develop thorough understanding of organisation and environment; emerges as nerve centre of internal and external information of the organisation	Handling all mail contacts categorised as concerned primarily with receiving information (eg, periodical news, observational tours)	Recognised in the work of SAYLES, NEUSTADT, WRAPP, and especially AGUILAR
Disseminator	Transmits information received from outsiders or from other subordinates to members of the organisation; some information factual, some involving interpretation and integration of diverse value positions of organisational influencers	Forwarding mail into organisation for informational purposes, verbal contacts involving information flow to subordinates (eg, review sessions, instant communication flows)	Unrecognised (except for PAPANDREOU discussion of 'peak coordinator' who integrates influencer preferences)

Role	Description	Identifiable activities	Status in the literature
Spokesman	Transmits information to outsiders on organisation's plans, policies, actions, results, etc; serves as expert on organisation's industry	Board meetings; handling mail and contacts involving transmission of information to outsiders	Generally acknowledged as managerial role
DECISIONAL			
Entrepreneur	Searches organisation and its environment for opportunities and initiates 'improvement projects' to bring about change; supervises design of certain projects as well	Strategy and review sessions involving initiation or design of improvement projects	Implicitly acknowledged, but usually not analysed except for economists (who were concerned largely with the establishment of new organisations) and SAYLES, who probes into this role
Disturbance Handler	Responsible for corrective action when organisation faces important, unexpected disturbances	Strategy and review sessions involving disturbances and crises	Discussed in abstract way by many writers (eg, management by exception) but analysed carefully only by SAYLES
Resource Allocator	Responsble for the allocation of organisational resources of all kinds – in effect the making or approval of all significant organisational decisions	Scheduling; requests for authorisation; any activity involving budgeting and the programming of subordinates' work	Little explicit recognition as a role, although implicitly recognised by the many who analyse organisational resource-allocation activities
Negotiator	Responsible for representing the organisation at major negotiations	Negotiation	Largely unrecognised (or recognised but claimed to be nonmanagerial work) except for SAYLES

Source: Mintzberg 1973
Table 7.1 Summary of Ten Roles

managerial functions called the *PRINCESS* factors (*Planning, Representing, Investigating, Negotiating, Co-ordinating, Evaluating, Supervising, Staffing*). GILLEN and CARROL (1985) in a study of 103 unit managers in ten industrial enterprises, again telescoped the *PRINCESS* factors to five: *Staffing, Planning, Investigating, Co-ordinating, Evaluating* and *Supervising* – inevitably called the *SPICES* categories.

Managerial roles
The most notable challenge to the domination of the functional approach in describing managerial jobs was mounted by MINTZBERG (1973), who developed his own typology for describing managerial work. He dismisses the functional approach (1975):

> 'If you ask a manager what he does, he will most likely tell you that he *plans*, *organises*, *co-ordinates* and *controls*. Then watch what he does. Don't be surprised if you can't relate what you see to these four words.
>
> The fact is that these four words which have dominated management vocabulary since the French industrialist HENRI FAYOL first introduced them in 1916, tell as little about what managers actually do. At best, they indicate some vague objectives managers have when they work.'

MINTZBERG, in research based on structured observations of five chief executives, proposed a new model of managerial work which is composed of ten work roles in three sets, as shown in figure 7.8. A definition of the roles is given in table 7.1.

Typical examples of these roles in the building organisation are:

1 **Figurehead** the managing director attending a topping out ceremony for a new building.
2 **Leader** a contracts manager responsible for motivating site managers, staffing new projects and training.
3 **Liaison** a buyer or marketing manager who establishes and maintains a network of outside contacts in the form of suppliers or clients respectively.
4 **Monitor** a strategic planning officer who conducts market research and organisational appraisal in the continuing process of developing strategies for the building firm.
5 **Disseminator** site manager transmitting information from architect to contracts manager, planning engineer, etc, for action.
6 **Spokesman** general manager speaking at schools career conference about the building industry and career opportunities.
7 **Entrepreneur** new business development manager seeking for opportunities for the building firm.

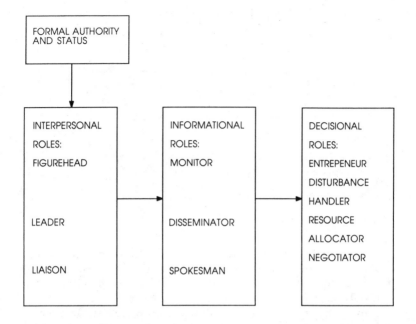

7.8   Mintzberg's ten managerial roles

8   **Disturbance handler**   industrial relations manager handling a strike on an important project.
9   **Resource allocator**   chief accountant allocating budgets to departments or divisions of the company.
10   **Negotiator**   director in charge of negotiating the acquisition of another company.

Not every manager fulfils all these roles but most building managers are engaged in most of them at various times in their career.

The roles do not form a logical sequential process as with the functions but rather an iterative cycle as shown in figure 7.9. A director of a building company may receive information (*Monitor*) at his golf club from a builders merchants' representative (*Liaison*) that a competing contracting firm is in financial trouble. He will then transmit this information to the board of directors (*Disseminator*) who may appoint the director to assess the opportunity for a takeover and the synergistic advantages to be obtained (*Entrepreneur*). He will seek further information about the ailing company either formally or, more likely informally (*Monitor*) using his network of contacts (*Liaison*).

The resource implications of the takeover will have to be carefully defined in terms of financial investment and commitment

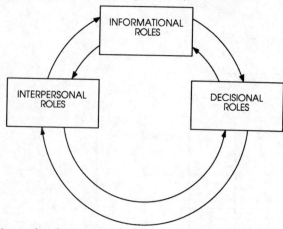

7.9   The cycle of managerial roles

of managerial time (*Resource Allocator*). Assuming approval is given to go ahead with the acquisition then the director will represent the company in negotiations with the competitor or the Official Receiver (*Negotiator*).

Any managerial job can be analysed in terms of these functions or roles. The conversion process within the management system consists of applying the functions or roles to the inputs of the task and the team.

Agendas and network building
Both the previous approaches make the job of the manager appear more systematic and predictable than it is in practice. Two further views by KOTTER (1982) and STEWART (1982) based on research suggests that managerial work is, as KOTTER says:

'. . . less systematic, more informal, less reflective, more reactive, less well organised, and more frivolous, than a student of management would ever expect.'

KOTTER goes on the explain this behaviour by explaining the two main dilemmas that most managers face:

1   'Figuring out what to do despite uncertainty, great diversity, and an enormous amount of potentially relevant information.
2   'Getting things done through a large and diverse set of people despite having little direct control over most of them.'

These two dilemmas seem particularly pertinent to construction managers who face uncertainty, diversity and information overload on construction projects which have to be completed with and through people over which he has little direct control, eg sub-contractors, the design team, etc.

An examination of efficient general managers by KOTTER suggests that they have developed an approach for handling the two dilemmas, the core of which consists of 'agenda setting' and 'network building'.

Agenda setting
KOTTER observes that general managers (corporate level) spend a considerable amount of the first six months to a year in post on establishing their agendas. Subsequently updating them is a less time-consuming process. Agendas consist of loosely connected objectives and plans that address long-, medium- and short-term responsibilities and address a broad range of financial, product/market, and organisational issues.

At the project level, a site manager may have less time, on a finite contract, to establish his agenda and it will focus on a narrower range of issues.

Although there may be formal planning processes at the corporate and project levels which produce written plans, the building managers' agendas will always include objectives, priorities, strategies and plans that are not in these documents. Formal plans and managers' agendas are not usually incompatible (although they may be), are generally very consistent but differ in focus. *First*, the agendas tend to be less detailed in financial objectives than formal plans and more detailed in strategies and plans for the business or project. *Second*, formal plans usually focus on the short to medium time horizon (three months to five years at the corporate level, less than five years at the project level), whereas managers' agendas tend to cover a wider time frame which includes the immediate future (one to thirty days) and the longer run (five to twenty years at the corporate level or the end of the project). *Third*, formal plans tend to be more explicit, rigorous and logical while agendas contain lists of objectives or plans that are not as explicitly connected or stated. Often the agenda items are not written down at all but remain mental maps in the manager's head. The process of setting the agenda consists of the early establishing of a rough agenda based on a limited knowledge of the business or project with subsequent incremental refining of the agenda as more information is elicited by informal contacts and questioning of people in the manager's 'network'.

Network building
As with agendas, managers spend considerable time early in their appointment establishing a network of contacts – people who will be helpful in implementing their emerging agendas. The network will include not just subordinates but peers, outsiders, their bosses' boss and their subordinates' subordinates.

Within the network the nature of the relationships will vary considerably in strength and significance and also over time, particularly, in building projects. People who will have a significant impact on the project in the early phases, eg the piling contractor, will be peripheral to the network at later phases of the project (unless there are problems of stability of the building due to the failure of the piling in which case the piling contractor will again assume a key role in the network).

These networks of cooperative relationships are developed by the manager using a variety of face to face methods, always trying to make others feel legitimately obliged to them by doing favours or stressing their formal authority. The network is used to implement the agenda either directly by ordering, asking, or suggesting to people in the network that they do something or indirectly by persuading a person in the network to get someone else to take the needed action.

The outcome of agenda setting and network building is that seemingly inefficient behaviour, characterised by activities that are brief, fragmented and frequently unplanned, is actually a very efficient and effective way of gathering up-to-the-minute information on which to base decisions. For example, an unplanned conversation between a contracts manager and one of his site managers, resulting from an accidental meeting, could involve the superior giving the subordinate a directive on a new project, finding out about the current status of an old project, learning about a potential problem arising from a current materials shortage, providing the site manager with advice on how to proceed on a project, discovering a possible way to implement an old plan, identifying a weakness in the site manager's assignment to a future project, and so on. A seemingly casual conversation between two managers can be a very efficient way of managing, enabling managers to get a lot of work done in very short periods of time.

Demands, choices and constraints

An alternative way of looking at the job of the manager with a view to improving its effectiveness has been provided by ROSEMARY STEWART (1982). As a result of research, she has developed a model with three important dimensions: the **demands** of the job, which are what the job-holder *must* do; the **constraints**, which limit what the job-holder can do; and the **choices**, which indicate how much freedom the job-holder has to do the work he chooses in the way he chooses. The model can be presented diagrammatically as shown in figure 7.10. The two diagrams represent two different and contrasting jobs. Job A imposes some demands on the job-holder, but allows considerable choice within broadly defined constraints. Typically jobs of this type in a building organisation might be marketing manager or contracts manager.

Job B makes heavier demands on the job-holder within tighter

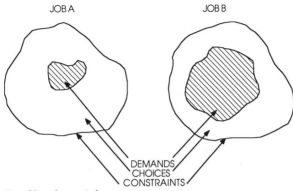

JOB A   JOB B

DEMANDS
CHOICES
CONSTRAINTS

7.10   *Profile of two jobs*

constraints thus narrowing the area of choice open to the manager. General foreman and plant managers may have a job profile of this type.
The nature of the demands, contraints and choices which managers face is shown in figure 7.11.

Demands of the job
Demands are what anyone in the job *must* do. They can be 'performance demands' requiring the achievement of certain minimum standard of performance, or they can be 'behavioural demands' requiring that you undertake some activity such as attending certain meetings or preparing a budget. ROSEMARY STEWART lists the sources of such demands as being:

- 'boss-imposed demands – work that the boss expects that the manager cannot disregard without penalty
- 'peer-imposed demands – requests for services, information or help from others at similar levels in the organisation. Failure to respond personally rather than delegate would produce penalties
- 'externally-imposed demands – requests for information or action from people outside the organisation that cannot be delegated and where there would be penalties for non-response
- 'system-imposed demands – reports and budgets that cannot be ignored nor wholly delegated, meetings that cannot be skipped, social functions that cannot be avoided
- 'subordinate-imposed demands – minimum time that *must* be spent with subordinates, eg guidance, appraisal, to avoid penalties
- 'self-imposed demands – by the expectation that you choose to create in others about what you will do; from the work that

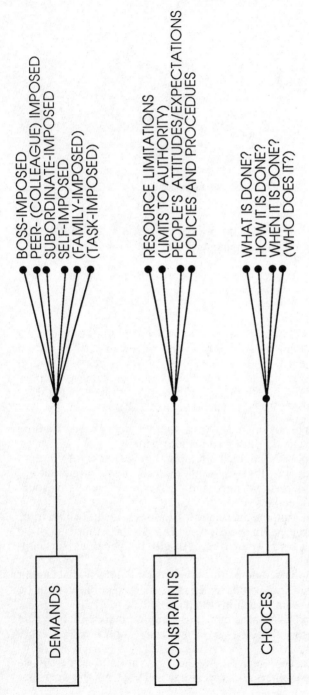

BOSS-IMPOSED
PEER- (COLLEAGUE) IMPOSED
SUBORDINATE-IMPOSED
SELF-IMPOSED
(FAMILY-IMPOSED)
(TASK-IMPOSED)

RESOURCE LIMITATIONS
(LIMITS TO AUTHORITY)
PEOPLE'S ATTITUDES/EXPECTATIONS
POLICIES AND PROCEDUES

WHAT IS DONE?
HOW IT IS DONE?
WHEN IT IS DONE?
(WHO DOES IT?)

DEMANDS

CONSTRAINTS

CHOICES

7.11 *Nature of demands, choices and constraints*

you feel you must do because of your personal standards or habits.'

2   Constraints

Constraints are the factors, both within the organisation and external to it, which limit what the manager can do. STEWART cites typical examples:

- (a) 'resource limitation, eg labour shortages on sites or finance available at the corporate level
- (b) 'legal regulations, eg Building Regulations, Companies Act, etc
- (c) union agreements, eg shifts or hours, extra payments
- (d) technological limitations – limitations imposed by trade processes or plant and equipment that can be used
- (e) physical location of the manager and his/her unit – the geographical distance of building sites from the company's Head Office frequently causes communications problems
- (f) organisational policies and procedures – may limit the authority of site manager to order plant or impose spending limits
- (g) people's attitudes and expectations – their willingness to accept, or tolerate what the manager wants to do, eg a decision to move the Head Office or to redistribute the workload of a contracts manager may meet resistance.'

3   Choices

All managerial jobs contain an element of choice. The area of choice may vary as shown in figure 7.10 but the main choices are:

- (a) choices in *what* is done
- (b) choices in *how* to do the work
- (c) choices in *when* the work is done
- (d) possible choices about *who* does the work.

For the site manager the choice about *what* is done may be limited by specifications, drawings and directions from the architect but the prototype nature of building means that there will be opportunities for suggesting alternative materials and techniques. The site manager will exercise considerable choice over method (how), timing within the limits of trade sequences (when), and has some discretion to give work to one person/gang or another. Equally, a director of the building company has extensive choice in all aspects.

Analysis of the manager's job using *demands*, *constraints* and *choices* can be very revealing, particularly if it leads to a recognition of the demands and constraints together with a realisation of the opportunities provided by choices.

An integrated model of the individual manager's job (CARROLL and GILLEN 1987) within the management system is shown in figure 7.12. This model integrates the four approaches – functions, roles, agendas and networks, demands, choices and constraints – into a single model of the manager at work. It also shows the inputs discussed in the previous section.

Some of the variables may cluster in particular ways to create managerial job types. MINTZBERG (1973) and STEWART (1967), have in particular, produced the lists of job types shown in figure 7.13 which they argue are discernible within the macro management system. The trend in thinking about managerial jobs has been away from the universal prescriptions of the functional approach towards recognition of the differences between managers jobs.

MINTZBERG 1973	STEWART (1967)
1 Contact man	1 The emissaries
2 Political manager	
3 Entrepreneur	
4 Insider	
5 Real time manager	2 The trouble-shooter
6 Team manager	
7 Expert manager	3 The writers
8 New manager	
	4 The discussers
	5 The committee men

Figure 7.13   Managerial job types

Macro level management process
The micro level conversion process exercised by individual managers is used to enable managers to fulfil the job types which comprise the macro management system. The micro level process and job types can occur at any level within the management system shown in figure 7.7. The 'Contact man' or 'Emissary' may be a salesman or a marketing director or even the chief executive. The importance of analysing the macro management system by strategic, co-ordinative and operating levels is that each level has a distinct orientation which does not necessarily correspond to the level in the hierarchy of the organisation. The site manager who is at the operating level may be making key strategic decisions if the project he is running will significantly affect the future of the building firm. Equally the chief executive may be involved in making operational project decisions in a large number of building organisations. The critical requirement is to recognise the level and consequences of the decision which is being made. The distinct orientation of the three levels of sub-systems within the management system are shown in figure 7.14.

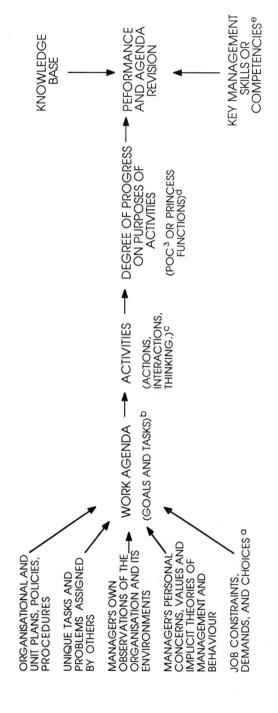

ORGANISATIONAL AND
UNIT PLANS, POLICIES,
PROCEDURES

UNIQUE TASKS AND
PROBLEMS ASSIGNED
BY OTHERS

MANAGER'S OWN
OBSERVATIONS OF THE
ORGANISATION AND ITS
ENVIRONMENTS

MANAGER'S PERSONAL
CONCERNS, VALUES AND
IMPLICIT THEORIES OF
MANAGEMENT AND
BEHAVIOUR

JOB CONSTRAINTS,
DEMANDS, AND CHOICES [a]

KNOWLEDGE
BASE

WORK AGENDA

(GOALS AND TASKS)[b]

ACTIVITIES

(ACTIONS,
INTERACTIONS,
THINKING.)[c]

DEGREE OF PROGRESS
ON PURPOSES OF
ACTIVITIES

(POC[3] OR PRINCESS
FUNCTIONS)[d]

PEFORMANCE
AND AGENDA
REVISION

KEY MANAGEMENT
SKILLS OR
COMPETENCIES[e]

[a] SEE STEWART (1982)
[b] SEE KOTTER (1982)
[c] SEE MINTZBERG (1973)
[d] SEE FAYOL (1949) AND MAHONEY, JERDEE, & CARROLL (1963)
[e] SEEKATZ (1974), BOYATZIS (1982), CARROLL & GILLEN (1984)

7.12   A model of the manager at work

The strategic management sub-system

The strategic sub-system, where ever it occurs within the organisation, is at the boundary of the organisation and at the interface with its environment. The orientation is predominantly *external* to the firm rather than internal and the focus is on decisions that are likely to effect the whole company. The greatest uncertainty and stress are faced by this sub-system with inputs that are unpredictable and which cannot be controlled. The strategic managers *must* adopt an *open systems* view in order to develop adaptable and innovative strategies.

Referring to figure 7.14 the role is to relate the organisation to its environment and to develop comprehensive systems and plans.

The nature of the strategic management job is that the environment faced is relatively open; the time perspective is long-term (three to ten years); the viewpoint is essentially one of satisificing – 'finding workable solutions to complex, unstructured, novel problems' (KAST and ROSENWEIG). Decision making is judgmental because decisions are 'unprogrammed' or non-routine.

The strategic system is discussed in greater detail in chapter 3, together with examples.

The operating management sub-system

The operating sub-system is the 'technical core' of the organisation which absorbs the majority of the firm's energy and attention. The objective at this level is to maximise the efficiency of the resource conversion process or, more plainly, to maximise the profit on current operations and projects. This is where the organisation derives the rationale for its existence – in the case of building organisations this means building structures and facilities on construction sites.

The efficient operation of the operating process usually requires that it proceeds in an uninterrupted way – that environmental influences are limited. Organisations therefore seek to protect and isolate their operating core, sealing it off by controlling inputs and outputs. The symbolic surrounding of the operating system by the strategic and coordinative systems shown in figure 7.7 is in practice what organisations seek to do.

To accomplish objectives efficiently and effectively as shown in figure 7.14 requires the allocation of resources between projects, the scheduling of operations, the supervision for performance and the control against the schedule.

The nature of the operating management job is that the setting is a relatively closed system for the reasons given above, although construction sites are likely to be rather more 'open' in the systems and physical sense than, for example factor production processes. The time perspective is short-term (weeks and months) with

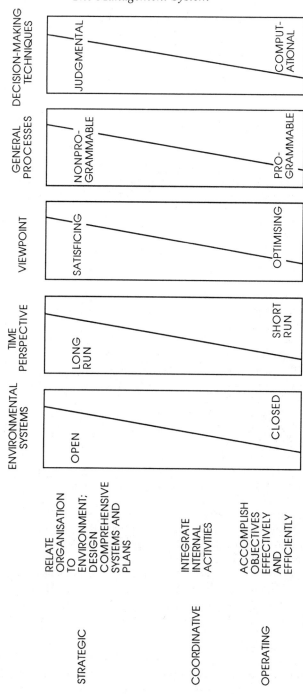

7.14 *The managerial task: strategic, co-ordinative and operating*

technical decisions that are optimal, programmed in the sense of being routine, and involve computational decision making using quantitative techniques. The majority of day-to-day site decisions will exhibit these characteristics but a significant proportion will have characteristics more reminiscent of the strategic level because of the nature of building operations.

This sub-system is covered in detail in chapter 16.

The co-ordinative management sub-system
The co-ordinative management role is to mediate between the strategic and operating systems to transform environmental uncertainty into operating predictability; and to structure resources to maximise performance potential of the firm. The sub-system achieves this objective through the integration of the internal activities of the organisation between functions and levels, and between projects and functions. It translates strategic plans into operating plans and procedures and interprets the results of the operating system into control data for the strategic system and for its own control systems.

The role of the co-ordinative system has two elements – organisation and resource acquisition and development. Organisation involves establishing authority and responsibility, workflows, information flows, distribution channels, and the location of facilities and services. This is discussed in chapter 4. The acquisition and development of resources (or inputs) – materials, plant and equipment, people, finance and facilities – are covered in detail in chapters 8 to 11. The co-ordinative sub-system has characteristics which are typical of both strategic and operating sub-systems.

Two further general points need to be made about the macro management systems.

First, the *size* of the organisation will determine the extent to which the strategic, co-ordinative and operating sub-systems are visible.

In small owner/management organisations the roles may be performed by a single individual; in larger organisations a clear hierarchy may exist which distinguishes the levels.

Second, the three sub-systems are not independent but rather interdependent. It is obvious from the previous discussion that the three sub-systems interact in a reciprocal way through directives and control processes.

7.5 Outputs

At the macro level the output of the management system is the performance of a set of *functions* which are required for the continuity of the organisation. These are strategic, co-ordinative and operational functions which must be fulfilled if the organisation is to survive; neglect of any of these functions will have a detrimental effect on the long-term health of the company. The failure of many building firms in the past can be traced to a neglect of strategic issues; these firms were often exceptionally efficient in the 'operational' and 'co-ordinative' (site and functional) areas of the business but failed to spot long term adverse trends that a proper attention to strategy could have highlighted. It is an axiom of business that companies with the wrong strategy, even if they are outstanding within their particular niche, are unlikely to survive in a rapidly changing environment. Conversely firms of only moderate efficiency who have the right strategy are more likely to survive and prosper.

The crucial issue is that a balanced attention to the performance of strategic, co-ordinative and operational outputs is critical to the long-term survival of the building organisation. This is the reason that specific chapters of the book have been devoted to the outputs of the various functions and levels that comprise a building firm. At the *micro* level of the management system the outputs are *decisions*, *assigning tasks*, and *providing support* that encourages performance. These activities form a set of outputs which individual managers perform in pursuing the *task* they have been set with the *team* that they have been given and within their own perceptions and style of *managing*.

Outputs are interelated in that decisions about what to do will effect who does it (assignment) and the consequent degree of support and facilities required. The outputs also form a logical sequence – decide what to do, give instructions, provide support.

A forth critical function is to check that the assignment is being or has been completed. This control loop is the feedback function within the management system which will be discussed in the next section.

Decisions

As discussed earlier, the decision making school of thought sees management as synonymous with decision making but it has been argued in this chapter that managers are involved in other activities as well. Nonetheless, decisions are a major output and decision making a central function of the management system.

ANSOFF (1965) identifies three classes of decisions – strategic, administrative and operational – which match the three types of tasks and the three levels of the macro-management system.

For the purposes of defining types of decisions as outputs it is more instructive to consider STEWART's (1982) analysis of the choices which managers have to make. Choices necessitate

decisions; if there is no choice there is no decision to make –
alternatives or options are the fuel which drives the decision making
system. Using this approach then decisions can be classified as
about:

(a)   What to do? (*Action*)
(b)   How to do it? (*Method*)
(c)   When to do it? (*Timing*).

This is a useful systematic framework for the types of decisions
which managers in building organisations have to make.

What to do (Action decisions)
Faced with an event, a crisis, a problem or an opportunity the
manager must first decide what to do, if anything. It is a legitimate
decision to do nothing if that decision is a positive one and not an
abdication of responsibility. A site manager may decide not to
intervene in a dispute over access to the crane between two sub-
contractors and allow the problem to be resolved by the parties
themselves. Before deciding what to do it has been suggested that
managers adopt a rational sequence of steps. These are:

(i)   Define the problem
(ii)   Analyse the problem
(iii)   Develop alternative solutions
(iv)   Decide on the best solution
(v)   Implement the decision.

The steps are self-explanatory but can be illustrated by reference
to a decision within a building company. As construction director,
you are concerned about an acrimonious dispute between one of
your site managers and the plant manager over the supply of plant
to site. The plant manager claims that the site manager is ignoring
company procedures which specify the use of requisition forms and
prescribed notice periods. The site manager is adamant that he
needs plant quickly to meet a changing construction programme
and that the plant department does not have sufficient plant and is
not flexible enough to meet the demand from sites.
    Having decided that a problem exists, investigation reveals that
the problem is the absence of proper programming of site activities
resulting in constant crises on the site; this is confirmed by the
materials purchasing manager who is facing similar problems on the
site. The investigation also reveals that the site manager is an ex-
bricklayer with little skill or interest in preparing programmes for
the work. As the company has no central planning department,
programming has always been the perogative of the site manager.
The construction director generates a number of potential solutions
to the problem. He realises he could dismiss the site manager and
replace him; send the site manager on a programming course;

appoint a planning engineer to plan this job and others; give the site manager a graduate building student to act as assistant and to do the programming, etc. He recognises there are constraints on the various options – the site manager is a long serving employee of the firm and well respected by site operatives. Equally, at fifty-five years old, he is unlikely to accept going 'back to school'. Appointing a planning engineer would entail interfering with successful programming practice on other sites in order to provide a full time job for the individual appointed as well as changing company policy. He therefore decides to appoint a building graduate from the local polytechnic course to act as assistant to the site manager and to take over the programming role. We can see that the decision about what to do is the termination of a sequence of explicit or implicit steps. The process may take months or seconds; it may be formally written down or completed entirely mentally.

How to do it (Method decisions)

Having decided what to do, the next step is to determine how to enact the decision. The construction director knows the head of the department of building at the local polytechnic through attending local CIOB centre meetings and telephones him explaining his requirements. The head of department is sure that, since programming is a major component of the course he will, after consulting the course director, be able to recommend a number of students for interview by the director. The head points out that, whilst interviews can take place immediately, the students will not be available until after their examinations in June – six weeks hence. This leads to the third type of decision.

When to do it (Timing decisions)

As the director feels that the selected decision is the best he is prepared to wait for six weeks to implement the decision. The contract is in its early stages so that there is plenty of time to introduce changes.

After the interviews the construction director will have to decide *who* is to fill the post of assistant site managers.

Assigning tasks

Having made a set of decisions about what to do, how and when to do the work, the logical next output of the management system is the assignment of tasks to particular people. Tasks can be assigned in two ways:

(a) in the form of a job description
(b) in the form of objectives.

Job descriptions
The traditional way of assigning tasks is to give a person a written description of the responsibility (demands) and constraints of the job; indeed this is a legal requirement as part of a Contract of Employment.

The job description approach to assigning tasks has been criticised on the grounds that responsibility for performing the task remains with the manager who has to exercise close and continual supervision to ensure that task objectives are met. It stems from Theory X assumptions about people (McGregor 1960).

A Theory Y approach to motivating people suggests that it is far better to assign tasks in terms of *objectives* to be achieved.

Management by objectives (MBO)
This approach, pioneered by Drucker (1954), is illustrated in figure 7.15 and is based on an entirely different philosophy to the job description method. The approach assumes that responsibility for methods of doing a job and performance should rest with the individual worker. The manager's role shifts from one of close supervision to that of agreeing organisational, departmental and individual job objectives (the ends), formulating measurable *action plans* to achieve the objectives in conjunction with the people involved (the means), allowing people to control their *own behaviour* and the activities required to implement the action plan, and *periodic reviews* of progress and performance in terms of the established objectives. This last step is fundamental to the success of the process.

An example of the MBO process would be a contracts manager meeting his site manager to agree the objectives for his current project. The objectives should be in a measurable form, eg stages of work to be completed by certain times, levels of materials wastage, bonus targets for various operations, etc, and will constitute action plans for the site manager. The contracts manager will then give the site manager time and opportunity to perform without close supervision. Periodic reviews (perhaps monthly) will assess progress and performance towards the agreed targets.

Providing support
The third output of the management system is action to support the people involved in undertaking tasks to enact the decisions taken by the manager. This support can be in tangible or intangible forms. **Tangible** support will be expected in the form of the necessary allocation of physical, financial and human resources to the task. 'Give us the tools and we will do the job' is not an unreasonable request and, as some motivation theories suggest (chapter 6), the lack of adequate resources is a great demotivator to people.

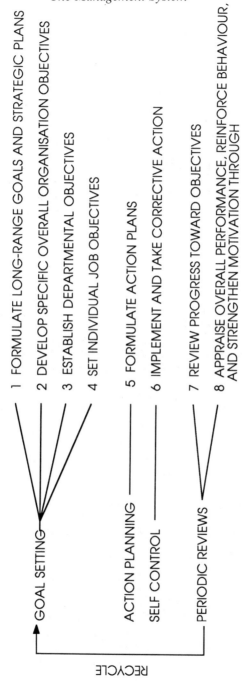

THE MAJOR STEPS

1 FORMULATE LONG-RANGE GOALS AND STRATEGIC PLANS

2 DEVELOP SPECIFIC OVERALL ORGANISATION OBJECTIVES

3 ESTABLISH DEPARTMENTAL OBJECTIVES

4 SET INDIVIDUAL JOB OBJECTIVES

5 FORMULATE ACTION PLANS

6 IMPLEMENT AND TAKE CORRECTIVE ACTION

7 REVIEW PROGRESS TOWARD OBJECTIVES

8 APPRAISE OVERALL PERFORMANCE, REINFORCE BEHAVIOUR, AND STRENGTHEN MOTIVATION THROUGH

A MANAGER TRAINING AND SELF-DEVELOPMENT
B COMPENSATION
C CAREER AND MANPOWER PLANNING

THE ESSENTIAL ELEMENTS

GOAL SETTING

ACTION PLANNING

SELF CONTROL

PERIODIC REVIEWS

RECYCLE

7.15 *The MBO process*

Construction sites abound with cases of operatives willing and ready to work but prevented from doing so by the lack of materials or equipment. Equally site managers often undertake major projects with derisory levels of staff support. At the corporate level directors must provide support to implement their policies and strategies.

Further evidence of tangible support is the provision of adequate and timely information (see chapter 5). The informational roles of the manager discussed earlier are concerned with this aspect.

Intangible support should be provided by the manager in the form of encouragement, guidance, or reprimand if necessary. The way in which this support is provided will depend upon the manager's style and his assumptions about what motivates people (see chapter 6). It is important that praise and reprimands are applied in a fair and balanced way. It is a feature of British managers, and construction managers in particular, that praise is seen as out of character so that only negative judgments are passed on a person's work. It is a key element of MBO that, during review sessions, the manager should deliberately stress the achievements as well as highlighting the short falls in performance.

7.6 The control loop

The feedback device in the management system is the control loop. This is shown in figure 7.16 in the systems context. The control

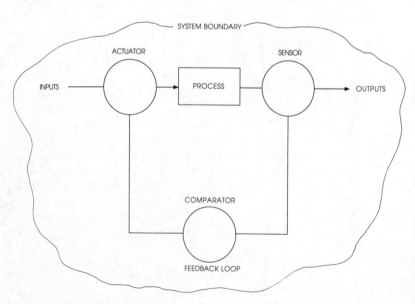

7.16   The control loop

process comprises a *sensor* to measure performance, a *comparator* to compare performance with some predetermined plan or standard, eg quantity and quality, and an *activator* which acts to correct any discrepancies or deviations from the target that are revealed by the comparison. Management by objectives as outlined earlier has all the ingredients of a good control system. The contracts manager in the example given will agree the objectives, the sensor will then be the periodic reviews together with any informal intelligence or symptoms gathered by the manager during his visits to site. Comparison of planned and actual performance can also be made during the review meetings and any corrective action agreed. Corrective action may require more support from the contracts manager as well as improvements by the site manager.

7.7 Summary

This chapter has reviewed the evolution of ideas about the role of the manager in the organisation and presented a model of the management system in terms of inputs, the conversion process and the outputs of the system.

As stated at the beginning of the chapter, the management system has a central role in integrating and directing the other systems shown in figure 1.4 and discussed elsewhere in the book.

Questions

1 Describe the process which may be involved in making and implementing decisions.
 Comment upon the importance of the quality of information in the decision making process.
 CIOB *Building Management I* (Resit) 1986

2 A general manager has been recruited by a regionally based building company. Identify the main issues with which he might concern himself during the first few months in his new position.
 CIOB *Building Management I* (Resit) 1986

3 The roles of a manager have been identified as relating to people, information and decisions.
 Analyse, within each of these three areas, the responsibilities of
 EITHER (a)   a building site manager,
 OR   (b)   a functional manager within a building organisation.
 CIOB *Building Management II* 1986

4 Rosemary Stewart has suggested that management jobs can be described and compared in terms of the demands, choices and constraints that the manager faces.

Use this framework to describe and compare the job of a site manager with that of a contracts manager.

References

Chapter 1

THE BANWELL REPORT (1964) *The Placing and Management of Building Contracts*, HMSO

CHANNON, D F (1978) *The Service Industries: Strategy, Structure and Financial Performance*, Macmillan

THE EMERSON REPORT (1962) *A Survey of Problems before the Construction Industries*, HMSO

KATZ, D and KAHN, R L (1966, 1978), *The Social Psychology of Organizations*, Wiley, New York

LANSLEY, P R *et al.* (1979), *Flexibility and Efficiency in Construction Management*, Ashridge Management College

LUPTON, T (1871), *Management and the Social Sciences*, Penguin

MILLER, E J and RICE A K (1967), *Systems of Organization: The Control of Task, and Sentient Boundaries*, Tavistock

NEDO (1978), *Construction for Industrial Recovery*, HMSO

NEDO (1983), *Faster Building for Industry*, HMSO

NEWCOMBE, ROBERT (1976), *The Evolution and Structure of the Construction Firm*, unpublished MSc thesis, University College, London

O'CALLAGHAN, J M (1986), *Managerial Characteristics and Financial Performance of Construction Companies*, unpublished MSc thesis, Brunel University

OGUNLESI (1984), *Strategy, Structure and Performance of Construction Firms*, unpublished MSc thesis, Brunel University

OPEN UNIVERSITY (1974), *People and Organizations DT 352 Unit 6:* The Organization as a System, Open University Press

THOMPSON, J D (1967), *Organizations in Action*, McGraw-Hill, New York.

Chapter 2

BENNETT, J (1966), *Constructions Project Management*, Butterworth

BURNS, T and STALKER, G H, (1966) *The Management of Innovation*, Tavistock

CLELAND, D I and KING, W R (1983), *Systems Analysis and Project Management* (3rd edn), McGraw-Hill

CIOB (1980), *Building for Industry and Commerce – A Clients' Guide*, CIOB.

CHERNS, A B and BRYANT, D (1987) 'Studying the Client's Role in Construction Management', *Construction Management and Economics*, Vol 2, No 2, Spon pp 177–184

HARDY, C B (1985), *Understanding Organizations* (3rd edn), Penguin Business Library

HARVEY, J (1987), *Urban Land Economics – The Economics of Real Property* (2nd edn), Macmillan

HIGGIN, G and JESSOP N (1965) *Communication in the Building Industry*, Tavistock Institute

HILLEBRANDT, P M (1974), *Economic Theory and The Construction Industry*, Macmillan

LANSLEY, P, QUINCE T and LEA, E (1979), *Flexibility and Efficiency in Construction Management*, Building Management Group, Ashridge Management Research Unit, February

LAWRENCE, R R and LORSCH, J W (1967), *Distribution of Influence in Two Organisations, Organisation and Environment*, Harvard

MACKINDER, M and MARVIN, H (1982), 'Design Decision Making in Architectural Practice', Institute of Advanced Architectural Studies, University of York, Research Paper No 19 April

NEDO (1970) *Large Industrial Sites – London*, HMSO

NEDO (1974) *Before you Build – What a Client needs to know about the Construction Industry*, HMSO

NEDO (1983) for Building EDC, *Faster Building for Industry*, HMSO

PERRY, T G and HAYES, R W 'Risk and its management in construction projects,' *Proc. Instn. Civ Engrs* Part 1 1985, June pp 499–521

POULIGUEN, L Y (1970), 'Risk Analysis in Project Appraisal', World Bank Staff Occasional Paper No 11, John Hopkins, University Press

RIBA, Plan and Work 1973, RIBA Publications

RICS and Dept of Construction Management, Univesity of Reading, UK and US Construction Industries, 1979, 'A Comparison of Design and Contract Procedures' RICS

THOMAS, P S October (1974), 'Environmental Analysis for Corporate Planning', Business Horizons pp 26–38

WALKER, A, (1984) *Project Management in Construction*, Granada.

Chapter 3

ANDREWS, K R (1980), *The Concept of Corporate Strategy*, R D Irwin

ANSOFF, IGOR (1965), Corporate Strategy, McGraw Hill

ARGENTI, J (1980), *Practical Corporate Planning*, George Allen and Unwin

AWAD, N I (1988), *Strategy Formulation Processes and Financial Performance in Construction Companies,* unpublished MSc Dissertation, University of Bath

BURGESS, R and WHITE, G (1979), *Building Production and Project Management*, Construction Press

CALVERT, R E (1981), *Introduction to Building Management*, Butterworth, London

CARLISLE, J (1987), 'Strategy and Success in the Construction Industry', *Managing Construction Worldwide*, Vol 2, Spon

CHANDLER, A D (1966), *Strategy and Structure*, Anchor Books, New York

CHANNON, D F (1978), *The Service Industries – Strategy, Structure and Financial Performance*, Macmillan

CYERT, R M and MARCH J G (1963), *A Behavioral Theory of the Firm*, Prentice Hall

DE BONO, EDWARD (1980), *Opportunities*, Pelican Books

FELLOWS, R F *et al.* (1983), *Construction Management in Practice*, Longmans

GLUECK W F *et al.* (1984), *Business Policy and Strategic Management*, McGraw Hill

GOLDSMITH, W and CLUTTERBUCK D (1984), *The Winning Streak*, Penguin

GRINYER, P (1972), 'Systematic Strategic Planning for Construction Firms', *Building Technology and Management*, February, pp 8–14

GRINYER, P *et al.* (1988), *Sharp Benders*, Basil Blackwell

JOHNSON, G and SCHOLES K (1988), *Exploring Corporate Strategy*, Prentice Hall

LANSLEY, P R *et al.* (1979), *Flexibility and Efficiency in Construction Management*, Ashridge Management College

LONDBLOM, C and BRAYBROKE D (1963), *A Strategy of Decision*, Free Press: New York

LONDBLOM, C E (1959), 'The Science of Muddling Through' D S Pugh (ed) *Organization Theory*, Penguin

MINTZBERG, H (1973), 'Strategy Making in Three Modes', California Management Review XVI, No 2 Winter

NEWCOMBE, R (1978), *Cost of Competition Building*

OXLEY, R and POSKITT J (1980), *Management Techniques Applied to the Construction Industry*, Granada Publishing

PETERS, T J and WATERMAN R H Jr (1982), *In Search of Excellence*, Harper and Row

PORTER, M E (1980), *Competitive Strategy*, Free Press

Chapter 4

ARGYRIS, C (1957), *Personality and Organization* , Harper and Row

BLAU, P M *et al.* (1976), Technology and Organization in Manufacturing, *Administrative Science Quarterly*, pp 20·40

BURNS, T and STALKER G M (1966), *The Management of Innovation*, 2nd ed, Tavistock

CHANDLER, A D (1966), *Strategy and Structure*, Anchor Books, New York

CHANNON, D F (1978), *The Service Industries: Strategy, Structure and Financial Performance*, Macmillan

CHILD, J (1984), *Organization: A Guide to Problems and Practice*, Harper and Row

CYERT, R M and MARCH J G (1963), *A Behavioral Theory of the Firm*, Prentice Hall

FAYOL, H (1949), *General and Industrial Management*, Pitman

FELLOWS, R F *et al.* (1983), *Construction Management in Practice*, Longmans

GALBRAITH, J R (1973), *Designing Complex Organizations*, Addison-Wesley

GREINER, L E (1972), 'Evolution and Revolution as Organizations Grow', *Harvard Business Review* July–August, pp 37–46

GRUMMITT, C N (1968), *The Mechanics of Construction Management*, Pergamon

HANDY, C (1981), *Understanding Organizations*, Penguin

HOMANS, G (1950), *The Human Group*, Harcourt Bruce, New York

IRWIG, H (1984), Organization Structures of General Contractors, *Organizing and Managing: Construction*, CIB, W-65

KAKABADSE, A *et al.* (1987), *Working in Organizations*, Gower

KAST, F E and ROSENZWEIG J E (1985), *Organization and Management* (4th ed), McGraw Hill

KHANDWALLA, P N (1977), *The Design of Organizations*, Harcourt Brace Jovanovich

KNIGHT, K (1976), Matrix Organization: A Review, *The Journal of Management Studies* pp 111–130

LANSLEY, P *et al.* (1974), *Management Style and Organization Structure in the Smaller Enterprise*, Ashridge Management College

LANSLEY, P R *et al.* (1979), *Flexibility and Efficiency in Construction Management*, Ashridge Management College

LAWLESS, D J (1979), *Organizational Behaviour: The Psychology of Efficient Management* (2nd ed), Prentice Hall

LAWRENCE, P R and LORSCH J W (1967), *Organization and Environment* Irwin

LIKERT, R (1967), *The Human Organization* McGraw Hill, New York

McGREGOR, D (1960), *The Human Side of Enterprise*, McGraw Hill, New York

MASLOW, A (1954), *Motivation and Personality*, Harper, New York

MAYO E (1945), *The Social Problems of Industrial Civilization*, Harvard University Graduate School of Business

MINTZBERG, H (1973), *The Nature of Managerial Work*, Harper and Row, New York

MINTZBERG, H (1979), *The Structuring of Organizations*, Prentice Hall

MINTZBERG H (1983), *Power In and Around Organizations*, Prentice Hall

O'CALLAGHAN, J M (1986), *Managerial Characteristics & Financial Performance of Construction Firms*, unpublished MSc thesis: Brunel University

OGUNLESI, Y (1984), *Strategy, Structure and Performance of Construction Firms*, unpublished MSc thesis: Brunel University

PATERSON, T T (1969), *Management Theory*, Business Publications Ltd

PERROW, C (1970), *Organizational Analysis: A Sociological View*, Brooks-Cole

PUGH, D S *et al.* (1968), 'Dimensions of Organization Structure', *Administrative Science Quarterly* pp 65–105

PUGH, D S *et al.* (1969), 'The Context of Organization Structures, *Administrative Science Quarterly* pp 91–114

RIBA (1973), Plan of Work, RIBA

SCHEIN, E (1980), *Organizational Psychology* (3rd ed), Prentice-Hall

STEWART, R (1970), *The Reality of Organizations*, Macmillan

STINCHCOMBE, A L (1959), 'Bureaucratic and Craft Administration of Production: A Comparative Study' *Administrative Science Quarterly* pp 168–187

STINCHCOMBE, A L (1965), 'Social Structure and Organizations', J G March (ed), *Handbook of Organizations*, chapter 4, Rand McNally

SIMON, H (1960), *The New Science of Management Decision*, Harper and Row

THOMPSON, J D (1967), *Organizations in Action*, McGraw-Hill

TRIST, E *et al.* (1963), *Organizational Choice,* Tavistock

WEBER, M (1947), *The Theory of Social and Economic Organization*, Free Press
WEINSHALL, T D (1971), *Applications of Two Conceptual Schemes of Organization Behaviour*, Ashridge
WOODWARD, J (1965), *Industrial Organization*, Oxford.

Chapter 5
BEC, CIOB (1986), 'Degrees in Building Management: Demand, Provision and Promotion', (The Lighthill Report), BEC/CIOB August
BENNETT, J, FLANAGAN, R and NORMAN G (1987), Capital and Counties Report: Japanese Construction Industry, Centre for Strategic Studies in Construction', University of Reading, May
BUILDING AND CIVIL ENGINEERING EDCs (1975), 'The Public Client and the Construction Industries,' (The Wood Report), HMSO
DEARDEN, J (1965), 'How to Organize Information Systems', *Harvard Business Review*, Vol 43 No 2, pp 65–73 March–April
FELLOWS, R F (1982), 'Cash Flow and Building Contractors', *The Quantity Surveyor* September
FELLOWS, R F (1982), 'Some Aspects of Contractors' Cash Flow', Department of Building Technology, Brunel University, Working Paper No 21, April
HANDY, C B (1985), *Understanding Organizations* (3rd edn), Penguin Business Library
JOINT CONTRACTS TRIBUNAL (1980), Standard Form of Building Contract – Private with Quantities, RIBA
KOONTZ, H, O'DONNEL C and WEIRICH H (1984), *Management* (8th edn), McGraw-Hill
NEDO (1983), *Faster Building for Industry*, HMSO

Chapter 6
BALES, R and SLATER, P (1955), *Role differentiation in small decision-making groups* Free Press
BAYLEY, L G (1973), *Building: teamwork or conflict*, Godwin
BOERCHERDING, J and OGLESBY C (1974), 'Construction productivity and job satisfaction', ASCE Construction Division, Vol 100, September
BORCHERDING, J and OGLESBY, C' Job dissatisfaction in Construction Work', ASCE Construction Division, Vol 101 June
BRAYFIELD, A and CROCKETT, W (1943), 'Employee Attitudes and employee performance', *Psychological Review*, No 50
BRESNEN *et al.* (1986), 'Leader orientation of Construction Site Managers', ASCE Journal of Construction Engineering and Management, Vol 112, No 3, September
CARNEGIE, J, (1975), *The nature and causes of casual employment in the building industry and the prospect for change*, MSc thesis Heriot-Watt, University
FIELDER, F, (1967), *A Theory of leadership effectiveness*, McGraw Hill
FLEISHMAN, E (1973), *Current developments in the study of Leadership in Twenty Years of consideration and structure*, Souther Illinois University Press
FORBES, W and MAYES, J (1969), 'The Output of Bricklayers', BRE Current paper 25/69
HANDY, C B (1976), *Understanding Organizations*, Penguin
HAYEL C (1973), *Encyclopaedia of Management*, Van Nostran Reinhold

HAZELTINE, C (1976), Motivation of Construction Workers', ASCE Construction Division, Vol 102, September

HERZEBERG, F (1957), *The Motivation to Work*, Wiley

KATZ, D and KAHN, R (1979), *The Social Psychology of Organizations*

LAWLER, E (1973), *Motivation in Work Organizations* Brooks/Cole

MARCH, J and SIMON, N (1961), *Organizations*, Wiley

MASLOW, A (1966), 'The Theory of Human Motivation', *Psychological Review* No 52

MASON, A (1978), 'Worker Motivation in Building', CIOB, Occasional Paper 19

MAYO, E (1949), *The Social Problems of an Industrial Civilisation*, Routledge

McGREGOR, D (1960), *The Human Side of Enterprise*, McGraw Hill

MEGGINSON, L, (1981), *Personal Management – a human resources approach Irwin*

MILLER D and FORM, W (1961), *Industrial Sociology*, Harper and Row

NEALE, R H (1981), *Municipal Building Management*, January

PHELPS-BROWN, E H (1968), Report of the committee of enquiry under E H Phelps-Brown into certain matters concerning labour in Building and Civil Engineering Command 3714, HMSo

PORTER L and LAWLER, E (1973), *Managerial attitudes and performance*, Brooks/Cole

REIMER J (1979), *Hard Hat – The Work World of the Construction Worker.*

ROETHLISBERGER, J M and DICKSON, H A, (1945) Management and the worker, Sage Harvard University Press

SAMUEL, P M (1971), 'Motivating employees', *Building Technology and Management*, March

SCHEIN, E H (1965), *Organizational Psychology*, Prentice Hall

SCHRADER, C (1973), 'Motivation of Construction Craftsmen', *American Professional Constructor*

SHENFIELD, B (1968), *Security of employment – a study in the construction industry*, PEP

STODHILL, R, (1974), *Handbook of Leadership*, Free Press, New York

SYKES, A (1969) 'Navvies – their work attitude', *Sociology*, January

TALBOT, P (1976), 'Financial incentives – do they work?', CIOB, Occasional Paper No 10

THOMAS, G (1963), *Operatives in the Building Industry*, HMSO

VROOM V and DECI, E, (1973) *Management and Motivation*, Wiley.

Chapter 7

ANSOFF, H IGOR (1965), *Corporate Strategy*, Penguin

ARGYRIS, C (1957), *Personality and Organization*, Harper and Row

BADDELEY, SIMON and KIM JAMES (1987), 'Owl, Fox, Donkey or Sheep: Political Skills for Managers',' *Management Education and Development*, Spring Vol 18 Pt 1

BELBIN, R M (1981), *Management Teams: Why They Succeed or Fail*, Heinemann

BLAKE, R R and MONTON J S (1968), *Corporate Excellence through Grid Organization Develoment*, Gulf Publishing Company

BRESNEN, M J *et al.* (1986), 'Leader Orientation of Construction Site Managers', *Journal of Construction Engineering*, Vol 112, No 3, September

CALVERT, R E, (1970), *Introduction to Building Management* Batsford

CAMPBELL, J P *et al.* (1970), *Managerial Behaviour, Performance, and Effectiveness*, McGraw – Hill, New York

CARLSON, S (1951), *Executive Behaviour*, Stockholm: Strömbergs

CARROLL, S J and GILLEN J D (1987), 'Are the Classical Management Functions Useful in Describing Managerial Work?', *Acad of Management Review*, Vol 12, No 1

CYERT, R M and MARCH, J G (1963), *A Behavioural Theory of the Firm* J J Englewood Cliffs, Prentice-Hall

DAVIS, R C (1951), *The Fundamentals of Top Management*, Harper and Row, New York

DRUCKER, P F (1955), *The Practice of Management*, Heinemann

FAYOL, H (1949), *General and Industrial Management*, London: Pitman

FEILDER, F E (1967), *A Theory of Leadership Effectiveness*, McGraw-Hill

GILLEN, D J and CARROLL, S J (1985), 'Relationship of managerial ability to unit effectiveness in more organic versus more mechanistic departments', *Journal of Management Studies*, No 22

GULLICK, L H and URWICK L F (1937) eds 'Notes on the theory of organisation', Papers on the Science of Administration, Columbia University Press, New York

HALES, COLIN, P (1966), 'What do managers do? A critical review of the evidence', *Journal of Management Studies*, Vol 21, No 2, pp 88–115

KAST F E and ROSENZWEIG J E (1979), *Organization and Management* (3rd ed), McGraw-Hill

KATZ, ROBERT L. (1955), 'Skills of an Effective Administrator', *Harvard Business Review*, January-February, pp 33–42

LIKERT, R (1961), *New Patterns of Management,* McGraw-Hill

MCGREGOR, D (1960), *The Human Side of Enterprise*, McGraw-Hill

Mahoney, T A *et al.* (1963), *Development of managerial performance: A research approach*, South Western, Cincinnati

MAHONEY, T A (1965), 'The job of Management', *Industrial Relations* No 4, pp 97–110

MINER, J B (1971), *Management Theory*, Macmillan, New York

MINER, J B (1982), *Theories of organization structure and process*, Dryden, Chicago

MINTZBERG, H (1973), *The Nature of Managerial Work*, Harper and Row, New York

MINTZBERG, H (1975), 'The Manager's Job: Folklore and Fact', *Harvard Business Review* 53(4), pp 49–61

SIMON, H A (1957), *Administrative Behaviour*, (2nd ed), Macmillan

STEWART, R (1967), *Managers and their Jobs*, Macmillan, London

STEWART, R (1974), 'The managers job: Discretion versus Demand', *Organizational Dynamics*, 2(3), pp 67–80

STEWART, R (1976), 'To understand the managers job: Consider demands and choices,' *Organizational Dynamics* 4(4), pp 22–32

STEWART, R (1982), 'A model for understanding managerial jobs and behaviour.' *Academy of Management Review* 7, pp 7–14

URWICK, L F (1952), *Notes on the theory of organization*, American Management Association, New York

URWICK, L F (1943), *The Elements of Administration*, Harper and Row, New York

URWICK, L F (1956), *The Pattern of Management*, University of Minnesota Press, Minneapolis.

Index